Egypt

by Sylvie Franquet & Anthony Sattin

Sylvie Franquet studied Arabic at the universities of Ghent, Tunis and Cairo, where she lived for six years, working as a model, translator and tour manager. She writes for the Belgian newspaper *De Morgen*. Anthony Sattin, a regular contributor on travel and literature to the *Sunday Times*, is the author of the *Pharaoh's Shadow: Travels in Modern and Ancient Egypt* and the *Gates of Africa: Death, Discovery and the Search for Timbuctoo*. He also discovered Florence Nightingale's *Letters from Egypt*. Together they have written several books for the AA (on Tunisia, the Greek Islands, Egypt, Bangkok, Brussels & Bruges, Morocco, and Istanbul).

Above: *brightly coloured wall-paintings in Gurna illustrate the family's daily life and pilgrimage to Mecca*

AA Publishing

Egyptian fellaheen
(farmers) still preserve
many of the traditions
inherited from their
ancestors

Written by Sylvie Franquet & Anthony Sattin

First published 2000
Reprinted Aug 2000
Reprinted Feb 2001
Reprinted 2003. Information verified and updated.
This edition 2005. Information verified and updated.
Reprinted Aug 2005

Published by AA Publishing, a trading name of Automobile
Association Developments Limited, whose registered
office is Southwood East, Apollo Rise, Farnborough,
Hampshire, GU14 0JW. Registered number 1878835.

A CIP catalogue record for this book is available from the
British Library.

A02738

Colour separation: Keenes, Andover
Printed and bound in Italy by Printer Trento s.r.l.

Find out more about
AA Publishing and the
wide range of travel
publications and services
the AA provides by
visiting our website at
www.theAA.com/bookshop

Contents

About this Book 4

Viewing Egypt 5–14

The Authors' Egypt 6
Egypt's Features 7
Essence of Egypt 8–9
The Shaping of Egypt 10–11
Peace and Quiet 12–13
Egypt's Famous 14

Top Ten 15–26

Abydos 16
El-Ahram and Abu'l Hol (Pyramids
  and Sphinx) 17
Biban el-Muluk (Valley of the Kings) 18
Deir Sant Katarin (St Catherine's
  Monastery) 19
Karnak 20–21
Khan el-Khalili, Cairo 22
El-Mathaf el-Masri (Egyptian Museum),
  Cairo 23
El-Nil (the Nile) 24
Philae Temples, Aswan 25
Sultan Hasan Mosque-Madrasa, Cairo 26

What to See 27–90

El-Qahira (Cairo) and Environs 30–49
In the Know 44–45
Alexandria, the Northwest and
  the Oases 51–63
Food and Drink 56–57
Nile Valley and Lake Nasser 65–83
Suez Canal, Sinai and the Red Sea 85–90

Where To... 91–116

Eat and Drink 92–99
Stay 100–05
Shop 106–09
Take the Children 110–11
Be Entertained 112–16

Practical Matters 117–24

Index and Acknowledgements 125–26

About this Book

This book is divided into five sections to cover the most important aspects of your visit to Egypt.

Viewing Egypt pages 5–14
An introduction to Egypt by the authors
    Egypt's Features
    Essence of Egypt
    The Shaping of Egypt
    Peace and Quiet
    Egypt's Famous

Top Ten pages 15–26
The authors' choice of the Top Ten places to see in Egypt, listed in alphabetical order, each with practical information.

What to See pages 27–90
The four main areas of Egypt, each with its own brief introduction and an alphabetical listing of the main attractions.
    Practical information
    Snippets of 'Did you know…' information
    1 suggested boat trip
    2 suggested walks
    3 features

Where To... pages 91–116
Detailed listings of the best places to eat, stay, shop, take the children and be entertained.

Practical Matters pages 117–24
A highly visual section containing essential travel information.

Maps
All map references are to the individual maps found in the What to See section of this guide.
For example, Abydos has the reference ➕ 29D3 – indicating the page on which the map is located and the grid square in which the site is to be found. A list of the maps that have been used in this travel guide can be found in the index.

Prices
Where appropriate, an indication of the cost of an establishment is given by **£** signs:

£££ denotes higher prices, **££** denotes average prices, while **£** denotes lower charges.

Star Ratings
Most of the places described in this book have been given a separate rating:
  ✪✪✪   Do not miss
  ✪✪   Highly recommended
  ✪   Worth seeing

Viewing
Egypt

The Authors' Egypt   6
Egypt's Features   7
Essence of Egypt   8–9
The Shaping of Egypt   10–11
Peace and Quiet   12–13
Egypt's Famous   14

Above: *a bright yellow sheikh's tomb in the Nile Delta*
Below: *a farmer uses age-old farming methods*

The Authors' Egypt

Change of Direction
The usual route for tourists in the past was to arrive in Cairo and then travel up the Nile to Luxor and Aswan. However, many people now head for the Red Sea coast or Sinai and make excursions to see the antiquities in Luxor, while more adventurous visitors are travelling further south along the Red Sea towards Sudan or making trips into the Western Desert. However, before setting off independently bear in mind that Egypt is still prone to security alerts (➤ 122, Personal Safety).

We were first drawn to Egypt for very different reasons. Anthony wanted to see some of the most fascinating relics of mankind's past, and I went to Cairo University to continue my Arabic studies, and to soak up the chaos and culture of the glorious city of Cairo. First we fell in love with the place, and later with each other, and we finally got married in a felucca on the Nile in the centre of Cairo. We have been going back regularly, as often as we can, now with two sons in tow, proving the Egyptian saying "Once you drink from the Nile you will always come back".

For us, Egypt has it all. With a long history behind and an uncertain future ahead, it is a fascinating country in flux. Signs of moving into the 21st century are everywhere but at the same time it is impossible to ignore that many *fellaheen* or farmers live a life quite similar to that of their ancestors. The monuments represent more than 5,000 years of history, and with so many so well preserved, there is always something new to explore.

Last but not least there are the Egyptians. After 2,000 years of foreign rule, they have preserved a lot of their unique physical and spiritual heritage. Despite their numerous problems they retain their strong sense of humour, and they somehow manage to laugh adversity in the face. We love it all.

Juice stall at Khan El Khalili marketplace in Cairo

Egypt's Features

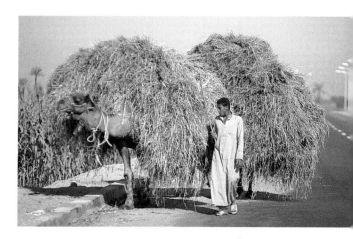

Egyptians

Egypt's 71 million inhabitants are a young community (almost half are under 20), some 90 per cent of whom are Muslims, the majority of the rest being Coptic Christians, with a small population of Jews and Christian denominations. Population movements have added to the racial characteristics of ancient Egyptians, exemplified in tomb paintings. Greeks and other Europeans in the north, the darker-skinned, distinctive features of Nubians in the south and the Semitic Arabs and Bedouins from the deserts to east and west have all had a marked influence.

The Land

Ancient Egypt was divided into red land (desert) and black land (valley and delta). About 95 per cent of Egypt's approximately 1 million sq km is desert, much of it lowlying, but also containing mountains, the highest being Gebel Katarina in Sinai (2,642m). The majority of the population lives on 33,000sq km of flat, fertile land irrigated by the Nile, which is intensively farmed.

Economy

Oil production, Suez Canal revenues, tourism and money sent home by Egyptian workers abroad account for the majority of foreign currency earnings. Some 29 per cent of Egyptians work in agriculture, 12 per cent of the workforce is unemployed, 15 per cent of jobs rely on tourism, 23 per cent of the population lives below the poverty line and 70 per cent live and work within less than 150km of Cairo.

Above: *many Egyptians still live off the land*
Below: *children are considered to be God's blessing*

Egyptians Abroad

Until the Gulf crisis of 1990–91, more than a million Egyptians worked in the Gulf. The money they sent home was crucial to the government and to their families. Their return to Egypt during the war created great social instability, but in recent years many have resumed work in the Gulf.

Essence of Egypt

Egypt boasts three of the greatest cities the world has known: pharaonic Thebes (Luxor), so important that the Egyptians simply called it 'the City', ancient Alexandria, the great centre of classical learning, and Cairo, Africa's largest city and legendary 'mother of the world'. Three deserts make up the bulk of the country, forbidding places that still fill most Egyptians with horror. The Nile, the world's longest river, runs straight through it, making the land habitable. Finally there is that unique, rich and sensual light, which endows Egypt and its people with a touch of brilliance.

Very few tourists venture out into Egypt's deserts, which make up most of the country

THE 10 ESSENTIALS

If you only have a short time to visit Egypt, or would like to get a really complete picture of the country, here are some of the essentials:

• **See the pyramids at Giza** (➤ 17) – they are, quite simply, wonders of the ancient world.

• **Sail the Nile on a felucca** listening to the water against the prow, the boatman's song and the sound of villagers along the shore.

• **Explore the varied, mineral-rich desert** which makes up more than nine-tenths of the country.

• **Snorkel or dive in the Red Sea** (➤ 89) to glimpse the corals and colourful fish, but remember to leave them as you found them.

• **Watch a belly dancer** to understand the sensual rhythm of the people and to tune your ear to the sounds of Egypt's traditional music.

• **Visit a mosque** – all but two of Egypt's mosques are open to tourists. Some are among the country's most stunning buildings.

• **Bargain in the *souks*,** remembering to pit your wits – and humour – against the salesman's wiles and hospitality.

• **Marvel at the pharaohs' treasures** in museums throughout the country, but especially in Cairo's Egyptian Museum (➤ 23) and the Luxor Museum (➤ 68).

• **Linger over a mint tea** or smoke a water pipe in a café for a glimpse into Egyptian daily life.

• **Get lost wandering around Karnak** (➤ 20–21), the ultimate expression of the power, the skills, the sense of beauty and religious fervour of the ancient Egyptians.

Sailing on a felucca between Aswan's islands at the end of a hot afternoon is totally relaxing

Belly dancing, probably originally a fertility dance, still holds a central place in popular Egyptian culture

The Shaping of Egypt

Early Dynastic Period (3150–2686 BC)
c3050 BC
Egyptian civilisation begins, when the land is unified by a semi-mythical king, known as Narmer or Menes.

Old Kingdom (2686–2181 BC)
c2649 BC
King Djoser is buried in the world's first all-stone building, the Step Pyramid at Saqqara (► 48–49).

c2566 BC
The Pyramid age reaches its pinnacle with the building of the Great Pyramid for Pharaoh Khufu. Over 2.3 million blocks of stone are used.

Middle Kingdom (2040–1782 BC)
2040 BC
Mentuhotep I reunites Egypt after 250 years of chaos and political disorder.

New Kingdom (1570–1070 BC)
1350 BC
Amenhotep IV (Akhenaten) and Nefertiti, his wife, abandon the old gods to worship the sun god Aten at a new capital, Amarna. After Akhenaten's death in 1334 BC, his successor Tutankhaten restores the old order and the old god

Amun, changing his own name to Tutankhamun.

1291–1278 BC
Seti I's reign is a high point in Egyptian art, as suggested by his temple at Abydos (► 16) and tomb in the Valley of the Kings (► 18). His son Ramses II boasted of his military prowess, but Egypt's empire is in decline.

331 BC
Alexander the Great founds Alexandria to bind ancient Egypt to the Mediterranean world. The dynasty created by his general, Ptolemy, rules Egypt until Cleopatra's suicide in 30 BC.

AD 45
According to legend, St Mark brings Christianity to Egypt. The Egyptian Coptic Church breaks links with other Christians in AD 451.

AD 641
Arab general Amr ibn el-As conquers Egypt, introduces Islam and sets up camp at Babylon (Old Cairo). The city of Cairo is founded AD 969, when Egypt is invaded by the Fatimids, a Shi'i sect from Tunisia.

1171–1193
The most famous of Egypt's medieval rulers, Salah ad-Din (Saladin), a

Kurd, liberates Syria and Jerusalem from the Crusaders and builds Cairo's Citadel (► 41).

1250–1517
The Mamelukes, Asian slave warriors, rule Egypt.

1517
Ottoman Turks invade and Egypt becomes a backwater in their empire. The route between Alexandria, Cairo and Suez becomes important as trade increases between Europe and the East. The British and French scheme to control it.

1798
Napoleon Bonaparte

leads a French expedition of soldiers and scholars to Egypt and stimulates the study and removal of antiquities.

1805

An Albanian mercenary, Muhammad Ali, takes power and begins to modernise Egypt. His sons and grandson continue the work, culminating in the redesign of central Cairo and the opening of the Suez Canal in 1869.

1882

The bankruptcy of the government and an uprising in the Egyptian Army are the pretexts of a British invasion, but British troops remain for the next 74 years.

1952

King Farouk is overthrown by army officers including Gamal Abdel Nasser, who becomes President. When Nasser nationalises the Suez Canal in 1956, he sparks a conflict with Britain, France and Israel. British troops finally withdraw.

1973

After several Arab-Israeli wars, both Egypt and Israel emerge from the 1973 conflict claiming victory. President Anwar Sadat negotiates the Camp David Peace Accord in 1979, which

Ismail, Muhammad Ali's grandson, believed that with the Suez Canal, Egypt belonged to Europe

returns Sinai to Egypt.

1981

Sadat is assasinated and Hosni Mubarak becomes President.

1997

Luxor tourist massacre by Islamic fundamentalists.

2004

Egyptian pound devalued to an all-time low. October bomb attack targets Israeli tourists in Taba.

Peace & Quiet

Urban Egypt can be a challenge to the senses and much of the coastline is crowded in summer, but there is no shortage of places where you can get away from it all.

The Nile

Some stretches of the river are busy with tourist boats, particularly in Cairo, Luxor and Aswan, but elsewhere the river is magnificent and makes a perfect retreat, particularly if you go on a silent felucca (➤ 78). Beyond the Aswan Dam, Lake Nasser is attracting a few more people in search of peace and quiet, but its vast expanse of water has hardly been disturbed (➤ 82–3). It is also home to massive fish (metre-long Nile perch are commonplace, while the largest recorded fish weighed some 200kg) and Nile crocodile, which haven't been seen north of the dam in living memory, but are reappearing in the lake.

Valley and Delta

You don't have to stray far from a road to discover peace in the countryside. Egyptian colours are straightforward – black earth, green crops and palm trees, blue sky and red sunsets (if you are lucky). As well as farmed animals, look out for egrets, hoopoes and scarab beetles, which, being the first creature to stir after the Nile floods subsided, symbolised resurrection to the ancient Egyptians.

El Faiyum

The colourful bee-eater overwinters in northern Africa; it favours hot, sheltered valleys with clumps of trees

Ancient Egyptians created a canal from the natural channel linking the Nile with the Faiyum (➤ 46) and its lake, Birket Qarun. Only an hour's drive from Cairo, it is a rewarding retreat in the desert. Until the early 20th century, Faiyum was a popular hunting ground and there are still duck and

many other wild birds, but as with the valley it is the peace of the farmland that is most refreshing.

The Deserts

Some 95 per cent of Egypt is desert and although the government has made great efforts to use it for mining, resettlement and, in the case of the new Toshka project, to green it, there is still plenty of empty space. Most of the Sinai peninsula (➤ 87–88) is desert, though of rocky plains and bare mountains rather than the sand dune variety. There is excellent birdwatching in spring and autumn along its western shore as migrating flocks navigate the Suez Canal. The Western or Libyan Desert, which includes the oases of Siwa, Bahariya, Kharga, Dakhla and Farafra (➤ 62–63), is becoming increasingly popular as a place of escape for Cairenes and their four-wheel drives, but still offers plenty of scope for peace. (Beware of going off-road alone. Always travel with at least three cars or take a good desert guide with you, ➤ 114). There is a good chance you will run into fennecs, snakes or see a bird of prey. The Red Sea mountains (➤ 90), between the Nile and the Red Sea, are mineral-rich and where the ancients cut gold, modern Egyptians extract phosphates and granite. Some of the earliest hermits came here for solitude and founded monasteries. In all the deserts, there is a chance of spotting jackals, snakes and scorpions.

Underwater

Snorkelling, or better still, scuba diving is about as peaceful an activity as you can do. Exploring Egypt's spectacular coral reefs is a pleasure for experienced divers as well as novices. Serious divers are heading nearer the Sudanese border to escape the polluting effects of tourism developments. For recommended dive sites, ➤ 89.

Sinai's mountains look barren, but the wadis and canyons contain enough water to sustain interesting wildlife

The Western Desert Oases are surprisingly rich in wildlife, including insects – such as this dragonfly at the Siwa Oasis

Egypt's Famous

Akhenaten and Nefertiti

Akhenaten (14th century BC), who was born Amenhotep IV, abandoned the state cult of Amun, the priests and court at Thebes to found a new capital at Tell el-Amarna called Akhetaten. He created his own religion, based on the worship of one god, the sun disc Aten, and revolutionised the character of Egyptian art by introducing a much more realistic style. Nefertiti, his wife, stands as an ideal of ancient beauty.

Tutankhamun

Akhenaten's only son, the nine year old boy-king Tutankhamun (died c1340 BC) returned the royal court to Luxor and reinstated Amun as state god after Akhenaten's heresy. He died in suspicious circumstances after a 9-year reign and lay almost undisturbed until Howard Carter opened his tomb in 1922.

Tutankhamun's golden funerary mask in Cairo's Egyptian Museum

Cleopatra

Cleopatra VII (69–30 BC) was banished from the throne by her younger brother Ptolemy XII, but she was reinstated in 47 BC when Julius Caesar came to Alexandria. Her name has become synonymous with seductive beauty – she had affairs with both Julius Caesar and Mark Anthony – but it is her suicide which sealed her fame, as she chose death rather than be taken in triumph to Rome. Look for her image at Dandara and in Alexandria's Graeco-Roman Museum.

Gamal Abdel Nasser

Nasser (1918–70) enjoyed success as one of the Free Officers who overthrew the monarchy and became Prime Minister and later the Republic's second president. He nationalised the Suez Canal and all manufacturing firms and financial institutions in order to finance the country's rapid industrialisation. Credited with building the Aswan Dam, he took responsibility for Egypt's defeat by Israel in the 1967 war. During his funeral in 1970 some 5 million people took to the streets.

President Hosni Mubarak

Hosni Mubarak (1928–) has been president since the assassination of Anwar Sadat in 1981. Although he has been admired for his steady handling of crises such as the Gulf War, fundamentalist violence and the great social changes currently sweeping Egypt.

Naguib Mahfouz

Naguib Mahfouz (born 1911), the grand old man of Egyptian letters, was awarded the Nobel Prize for Literature in 1988. *The Cairo Trilogy*, partly auto-biographical, is set in the Cairo of his childhood in the early 1900s and is told in the style of the great European novelists. Most of his novels are set in Islamic Cairo and Alexandria.

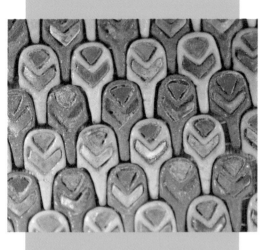

Top Ten

Abydos 16
El-Ahram and Abu'l Hol
    (Pyramids and Sphinx) 17
Biban el-Muluk
    (Valley of the Kings) 18
Deir Sant Katarin (St Catherine's
    Monastery) 19
Karnak 20–21
Khan el-Khalili, Cairo 22
El-Mathaf el-Masri
    (Egyptian Museum), Cairo 23
El-Nil (the Nile) 24
Philae Temples, Aswan 25
Sultan Hasan
    Mosque-Madrasa, Cairo 26

Above: *detail of fine enamelled jewellery found
inside Tutankhamun's tomb*
Right: *wall-painting of ancient Egyptians making
offerings to their gods*

15

1
Abydos

✚ 29D3

✉ El-Araba el-Madfuna,
10km south-west of el-
Balyana

🕐 Daily 8–5 (4 in winter)

🍴 Café (£) opposite
temple entrance

🚌 Luxor travel agency
excursions and taxi are
the preferred ways to
get to Abydos

🚂 Train connections from
Cairo and Luxor

✋ Cheap

↔ Dandara (➤ 74) if
travelling from Luxor,
Sohag (➤ 75)

❓ Check security
arrangements before
travelling

*The reliefs found in
Seti I's temple at Abydos
are some of the most
beautiful and exquisite in
Egypt*

*Abydos, dedicated to the god Osiris, was a place of
pilgrimage for almost two thousand years. Today
it is one of the most remarkable archaeological sites.*

Abydos is one of the oldest Egyptian settlements, founded
long before the Dynastic period (3050 BC), and for
thousands of years it was a place of pilgrimage. According
to legend, Osiris, god of the underworld, was buried here,
and a gap in the nearby hills was the gateway to the underworld. A burial in Abydos, therefore, was considered a
good way of ensuring an after-life. Early Egyptian kings
built symbolic graves in the desert and those who could
were either buried there, had commemorative stones
raised in their honour or had their mummies brought on
pilgrimage after their death.

Most of ancient Abydos has disappeared or is yet to be
excavated. The main attraction is the Temple of Seti I, a
magnificent white-marble building of the 14th century BC.
There are many inscriptions and images, while reliefs on
the walls of the Second Hypostyle Hall are among the
finest of the New Kingdom, with a subtlety and vividness
that was later lost. The temple's outer hall and façade
were finished by Seti's son, Ramses II, who also built a
smaller temple some 300m away (not always accessible).
Before visiting that, however, go out of the back of the
temple to the Osirion or Cenotaph, a strange subterranean
building, now often submerged by rising ground-water. A
sarcophagus was found here (although Seti was buried in
the Valley of the Kings, ➤ 18), which was perhaps part of
a ritual unification of the pharaoh and the god of the dead.

2
El-Ahram & Abu'l Hol
(Pyramids & Sphinx)

The pyramids at Giza are the most instantly recognisable monuments in the world, while the nearby Sphinx retains its aura of mystique.

The sound and light show gives an insight into the story of King Khufu

More than 80 pyramids line the west bank of the Nile between Giza and El-Faiyum, but the three large pyramids at Giza are by far the most impressive. It is easy to trace the fascinating development of the pyramids from the beginning with Djoser's Step Pyramid at Saqqara (► 48), through Snefru's pyramids at Dahshur (► 46) to the geometrically perfect Great Pyramid of Khufu (Cheops), built at the apogee of Old Kingdom power. Khufu's was the first of the three main pyramids to be built and is the largest, originally 146.6m high (now shrunk to 137.5m) and built out of 2,300,000 blocks weighing an average of 2.5 tonnes each. His son Khafre (Chephren) built the Second Pyramid (136.4m high) and gave the Sphinx his face, while Khafre's son Menkaure (Mycerinus) built the third, only 62m high. Around each pyramid there are the remains of the smaller pyramids of the royal families.

If there is still no complete answer to the question of how the pyramids were built, then the Sphinx is shrouded in even more mystery. The massive statue cut out of the living rock has a lion's body, and a man's head, believed to be that of the Pharaoh Khafre, to whose pyramid it was connected by a causeway. In order to protect the Giza plateau, it is being surrounded by a wall, which in 2005 will only leave one entrance to the site, on the El Faiyum-Cairo road. Plans are also under way for a new and larger Egyptian Antiquities Museum on the edge of the plateau.

✚ 28C4

✉ Giza plateau, 16km southwest of Cairo

🕐 Site daily 8–4 (8–5 summer); interior of Great Pyramid 8:30–3:30

🍴 Café (£) near Sphinx, restaurant (££–£££) at Mena House Hotel

🚌 900 and 80, minibus 82

ℹ Opposite Mena House Hotel ☎ 02-385 0259

💷 Expensive to enter the site and the Pyramid of Khafre, extra ticket expensive to enter the Pyramid of Khufu and moderate to enter the Pyramid of Menkaure

↔ Solar Boat Museum (► 47)

❓ *Son et lumière* show in several languages at the Sphinx daily ☎ 02-385 2880 for information

3
Biban el-Muluk
(Valley of the Kings)

The secluded valley of the New Kingdom was known as the 'place of truth'

For 500 years some of Egypt's most famous pharaohs were buried in splendour in fascinating tombs in the Valley of the Kings.

One of the high points of ancient Egyptian history occurred when the princes of Thebes (Luxor) established what is known as the New Kingdom (1570–1070 BC). Previous pharaohs had been buried in pyramids, which had proved easy to rob. Theban pharaohs, who believed their future life depended on keeping their mummies and grave goods intact, had themselves buried in the hills. The tombs were literally cut out of the rock and some are masterpieces of engineering: Seti I's tomb is 100m long, while KV5, the tomb of the sons of Ramses II has so far revealed more than a hundred chambers. The walls were covered with inscriptions and decorations, many of which were there to instruct the pharaoh on how to reach the underworld. The tombs were filled with gold and precious objects, protected by deep pits and hidden beneath the valley's rubble. All were broken into in antiquity.

Seti I's tomb is considered to be the finest in the valley, by those who have been lucky enough to see it – it is usually closed (Horemheb's No 57 is similar in design if not decor). Tombs are regularly closed and numbers are often restricted, as in Tutankhamun's, to minimise damage. The boy-king's tomb is of interest because of the romance surrounding its discovery and because the mummy is still there. After the tomb was opened by Howard Carter in 1922, several people who visited the site or were involved in its discovery died mysteriously, said to be caused by the curse of the pharaoh.

Amongst the more heavily decorated tombs are those of Ramses IV (No 2), Ramses VI (No 9), and Ramses III (No 11), while that of Tuthmosis III (No 34), high up the valley, is the most challenging to reach.

29D2

West Bank, beyond el-Gurna

Daily 7–4 (7–5 in summer)

Café (£) at the valley entrance

Taxis only, or rented bicycles

Corniche el-Nil, Luxor
☎ 095-372215

Moderate; expensive for Tutankhamun

Deir el-Bahri (➤ 70), Ramesseum (➤ 73)

Ticket office at the crossroads after the Colossi of Memnon, where you will be told which tombs are open for the public

4

Deir Sant Katarin (St Catherine's Monastery)

The monastery is holy to Jews, Christians and Muslims, and is built on the site where Moses is believed to have received the Ten Commandments.

29D4

Sinai desert, 450km from Cairo, 140km from Dahab

Head office: St Catherine Protectorate 062-470 032, fax 062-470 033

Mon–Sat, Sat 9-12. Closed Sun and religious holidays

Café/restaurant (£)

Buses from Cairo, Sharm el-Sheikh, Dahab and Nuweiba to the village, 2km from the monastery. Taxi to monastery or pleasant walk

Air Sinai flights to St Catherine's from Cairo

Few

Free

Good guidebook and local walking guides available at the monastery. Special permission needed to visit the Chapel of the Burning Bush

According to the scriptures, when Moses went up towards Mount Sinai to receive the Ten Commandments, God spoke to him through a burning bush. The monastery was founded on the supposed site of the bush in AD 527, on the orders of Byzantine Emperor Justinian. Unlike other monasteries in Egypt, St Catherine's belongs to the Greek Orthodox Church and is rich in traditions, one being to hide most daily rituals from visitors. The monastery's icon collection is one of the most important in the world, covering 1,400 years of painting, including the period when Byzantine Christians were banned from producing images of the Holy Family or saints (AD 746–842) – an injunction that isolated Sinai ignored.

Icons are shown in the narthex of the main church, an original Justinian granite building that incorporates the Chapel of the Burning Bush. Inside the church, through wonderful 6th-century cedarwood doors, icons of the saints are hung on and around twelve magnificent pillars and candles are lit under their images on their name day. The iconostasis (altar screen) is a later 17th-century work, but beyond it in the sanctuary there is one of the masterpieces of Byzantine art, a 6th-century mosaic of the Transfiguration. Outside the church a bush grows which, in spite of local legend, is not the one mentioned in the Bible.

The exceptional 6th-century mosaic of the Transfiguration of Christ was executed like a painting

19

5
Karnak

🔲 29D3

✉️ 2.5km north of Luxor centre

🕐 Daily 6–5:30 (open till 6:30 in summer)

🍴 Café (£) by the Sacred Lake

🚌 Minibuses from Luxor centre

ℹ️ Corniche el-Nil, Luxor ☎ 095-372215

✋ Moderate

↔️ Luxor Temple (➤ 67), Luxor Museum (➤ 68), Mummification Museum (➤ 68)

❓ *Son et lumière* show (a walking tour of the temple) 3 or 4 times daily (recommended)

Opposite: *the towering columns of the hypostyle hall*
Below: *the Processional Way, lined with ram-headed sphinxes*

No other ancient religious centre matches Karnak for scale and grandeur. Here, for 1,500 years, the priests offered prayers to the god Amun.

Amun was the local god of Thebes long before the New Kingdom, but his status grew along with that of the Theban princes. By the end of the New Kingdom the priests of Amun owned huge estates and controlled shipping, farming and industry. Their empire within an empire was controlled from the precinct of Amun in Karnak and at its centre stood the temple, embellished over the centuries as pharaohs wished to show goodwill towards the god. The result is one of the world's most extraordinary religious sites.

Karnak is a complex with several temple compounds, which can be confusing and overwhelming to visit. After entering through the 43m-high outer pylon, walk to the core of the complex, the Temple of Amun. Dedicated to the triad of Thebes, the gods Amun, Mut and Khonsu, it has a wonderful 'forest' of pillars, built by Ramses II. Continuing straight through the halls you will come to the sanctuary where the image of Amun lived and where, as the images on the walls show, daily offerings were made. Retracing your steps, turn left out of the inner sanctuary to the Cachette Court, where a massive cache of statues was found, and continue to the Sacred Lake. From here, on the *son et lumière* stand, you can see over the compound. If you have time, stroll through the Open Air Museum, the Northern Enclosure with the Temple of Mut, and the Southern Enclosure.

6
Khan el-Khalili, Cairo

The warren of alleys brings a touch of the Arabian nights to Cairo, in which shopping is just part of the sensory adventure.

The original *khan* (merchants' inn and storehouse) was built in 1382 and quickly became the focus of the city's international trade. Although it was reconstructed in the 16th century something of the spirit of the original place is still there, as people from all over the world meet to talk and trade.

Officially Khan el-Khalili now refers to a single street, but generally it is used for the shopping area between the Mosque of Sayyidna el-Husayn (➤ 43) and Muizz lidin Allah, one of the Islamic city's main streets. The main alley connecting them, el-Badestan, is typical with its mix of cheap souvenirs and treasures, where imported Chinese junk sits alongside expensive jewellery and Lalique glass. In a smaller alley to the left of el-Badestan, coming from el-Husayn, Fishawi's café claims not to have closed since 1773 – not quite true, as you might find, but it is one of the area's social centres.

In the alleys of the Khan el-Khalili there are silversmiths, copper beaters, leather workers and carpet sellers. At the bottom of el-Badestan, turn right onto the street of Muizz lidin Allah, which leads to the old *souk* el-Nahassin (the copper and gold market) where you can buy wonderful copper trays and gold jewellery. Heading the other way along this extraordinary street, past the old baths, an alley running alongside the Mosque of Barsbay leads past kohl and perfume sellers to the spice market.

33D4

Off Sharia el-Azhar and Sharia el-Muski

Morning to evening (many shops closed Fri prayers and Sun)

Several cafés and restaurants (£–££)

Buses from Midan Tahrir

5 Sharia Adly, Downtown
☎ 02-391 3454

El-Azhar (➤ 34), Bayt el-Suhaymi (➤ 36), Mosques of Qalawun, El-Nasir and Barquq (➤ 41), Sayyidna el-Husayn (➤ 43), Wikalat el-Ghuri (➤ 43)

The cafés around Midan el-Husayn are popular in the evening for a mint tea or a waterpipe; the bazaar is especially crowded during *moulids* (➤ 116)

Watch the world go by from a café terrace

7

El-Mathaf el-Masri
(Egyptian Museum), Cairo

The Egyptian Museum is one of the world's great storehouses of antiquities, and a visit is essential for understanding the glory of the ancient Egyptians.

www.egyptianmuseums.gov.eg

✚ 32B4

✉ Midan el-Tahrir, Cairo

☎ 02-575 4319

🕐 Daily 9–6

🍴 Several restaurants and cafés outside the museum (£–£££)

Ⓜ Sadat

🚌 Many buses to Midan Tahrir

♿ Few

✋ Moderate; video permission very expensive; royal mummies expensive–very expensive

↔ Gezira (➤ 37)

Only part of the museum's collection is on display, but what there is to see is more than anyone could take in on a single visit, so save time to return. The ground-floor galleries are laid out in rough chronological order (though unfortunately not numerically, No 1 is not the oldest), allowing you to walk clockwise from the entrance and have an overview of three thousand years of Egyptian art. Immediately in front of the entrance there is a changing exhibition of masterpieces and in the central atrium gallery there are monumental pieces, including pyramid tops and a magnificent Amarna floor.

The upper floor is devoted to treasures, most of them found in tombs. The staircase in gallery 1 leads directly into the most popular collection, the unique treasures of Tutankhamun. Here, filling several galleries, are the 1,700 grave goods found in his tomb, from the solid gold mask to thrones, headrests, exquisite boxes and a series of golden chariots. The Tutankhamun treasures can overwhelm, but save some energy for other galleries, which are arranged according to subjects, from models (boats, farming scenes, warriors) to the lifelike Graeco-Roman portraits (room 14). The mummies of several important pharaohs, including Ramses II, are on show in room 52 (separate ticket required). Plans for a larger, high-tech Egyptian Museum on the Giza Plateau are on their way but the project will not be complete for a few years.

Left: *beautiful jewellery from the treasure of Tutankhamun*
Below: *the amazing golden death mask of the boy-king Tutankhamun*

8
El-Nil (the Nile)

Cruises on the Nile
A variety of boats sail on the Nile, from simple feluccas to five-star cruise-boats, but most offer the same itinerary. Sailing between Luxor and Aswan, they take in the sights in both towns and stop at the temples of Esna, Edfu and Kom Ombo on the way. Most cruises take three or four days, although some take five and visit the temple of Dandara. A few boats make the trip from Cairo, which takes 10 days. Delays may occur at the narrow Esna lock, where boats often have to join a long queue waiting to pass through, so some companies transfer passengers to a sister boat waiting on the other side.

Herodotus' claim that Egypt is a gift from the Nile is still valid today

This great river may no longer be Egypt's communication nerve, but it is still the country's lifeline and one of the things that draws people here.

The Nile is the world's longest river and one of the most beautiful. For the last half of its course it receives neither tributaries nor regular rainfall yet in midsummer every year it used to rise in Egypt until it burst its banks and flooded the valley. Villages were built on mounds and ancient writers described them as looking like islands. When the river finally subsided it left a thick deposit of mud on the land, producing fertile ground on which seeds were immediately planted. Some years the river rose so high it destroyed villages and towns, while in others it didn't rise high enough to produce a good crop and people went hungry. Ancient Egyptians worshipped the Nile as a god and hoped for its benevolence.

The source wasn't discovered until the 1850s, when the British explorers Burton and Speke reached Lake Victoria. As a result of knowledge gained about the river, two dams were built (1902 and 1965) to control the flow of water to the valley. The dams and the resultant Lake Nasser, the world's largest reservoir, have ended the flooding and made several crops a year possible, although the farmland is now suffering from a lack of fertilising silt. With the Nile tamed, river travel now almost exclusively for tourists and more people moving from the country to the city, it is tempting to think that the river no longer has significance, but the Nile is as much a part of Egyptian life now as it was in ancient times.

9
Philae Temples, Aswan

Philae reveals the glory of ancient Egypt's late flourish under the Greeks and Romans. It is also one of Egypt's most romantic sites.

➕ 29D2

✉ Agilkia Island, 9km south of Aswan

🕐 Daily 7–4 (7–5 in summer)

🍴 Café (£) on the shore

🚌 Taxi from Aswan

🚤 Regular boats from the riverbank

ℹ Corniche el-Nil, Aswan ☎ 097-312 811

✋ Moderate–expensive

↔ Aswan Dam (➤ 79)

❓ Daily *son et lumière* show (recommended). Details at the site or tourist office

The temples, shrines and kiosks of Philae Island were moved to the nearby Agilkia Island between 1972 and 1980 to protect them from the rising Nile water caused by the Aswan dams. As part of the massive operation Agilkia was shaped to make a convincing replica of Philae Island. The main temple at Philae was dedicated to Osiris's wife Isis, who was worshipped throughout the Mediterranean world in Roman times and whose cult survived here until AD 551, when it was replaced by that of the Virgin Mary.

Arriving at the island by boat is a wonderful experience. From the landing, long colonnades lead up to the pylon of the Temple of Isis, which was built during the late Ptolemaic and early Roman era. The left-hand opening leads into a 3rd century BC Birth House, dedicated to Horus, child of Isis and Osiris. The main opening leads to a second pylon and the temple, which lost much of its decoration when it was converted into a church around AD 553. The upper floor has interesting reliefs of Osiris, who was worshipped in mysterious rites here. The nearby Temple of Hathor, the deity associated with music, has a unique image of gods playing instruments. From the Kiosk of Trajan, originally built as a gateway to the island, there are beautiful views across the lake to the site of the original island, now submerged.

Trajan's Kiosk with its marvellous carved columns was designed as the formal entrance to the island

10
Sultan Hassan Mosque-Madrasa, Cairo

✝ 33C3

✉ Midan Salah el-Din

🕐 Daily 8–5 (open till 6 in summer)

🍴 Open-air café (£) next door (summer only)

🚌 54 from Midan el-Tahrir

✋ Moderate

↔ Bayt el-Kritliya (➤ 36), Citadel (➤ 41), Ibn Tulun Mosque (➤ 37)

The simple beauty and grand scale of this 14th-century mosque make it one of the most admired of Islamic monuments.

Sultan Hassan was the seventh of Sultan el-Nasir Muhammad's eight sons and was 12 years old when he became sultan of Egypt in 1347. Four years later he was imprisoned in the *harem* by a younger brother. After three years of *harem* life, he was restored to the throne, where he stayed for nearly seven years before being murdered. In his life he knew wealth and debauchery, but Sultan Hassan will always be remembered for his teaching mosque (*madrasa*), one of the largest and finest in the world.

The mosque was the centre of the community, accommodating students of four separate schools of Islamic law. The original design had four minarets but only three were built. One fell in 1361, killing many people; another fell in 1659 and was replaced by a smaller minaret. The sole survivor is 81.6m high, one of the tallest in the city. The sultan intended to be buried here, but the tomb is empty, as his body disappeared. The tomb chamber is decorated with marble and wood, with a blue and gold wooden frieze around the room. The masterpiece, however, is the main prayer space, a massive, perfectly proportioned courtyard with four huge arches leading off it in symmetry, creating four open-sided rooms. Between them are doors to the law schools and, at the centre, a domed fountain for ablutions. Beautiful glass lamps (some now in the Museum of Islamic Art, ➤ 38) were used to illuminate the prayer recesses.

The best time to view Sultan Hassan's mosque-madrasa is in the morning, when the sun lights up the mausoleum and the courtyard

What to See

El-Qahira (Cairo) and
  Surroundings   30–49
In the Know   44–45
Alexandria, the Northwest
  and the Oases   51–63
Food and Drink   56–57
The Nile Valley and Lake
  Nasser   65–83
Suez Canal, Sinai and the
  Red Sea   85–90

Above: *the alabaster sphinx staring over the ruins of Memphis*
Right:*a visit to the Coptic Museum is a must*

27

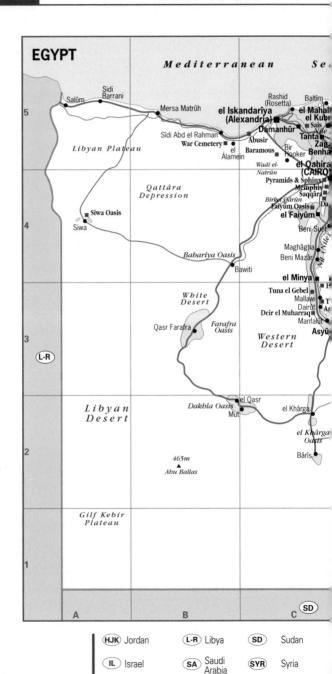

EGYPT

Mediterranean Se

Salûm • Sidi Barrani • Mersa Matrûh

Rashid (Rosetta) • Baltim
el Iskandarîya (Alexandria) • el Mahal • el Kubr
Sais • Aîle
Dâmanhûr • Tanta • Zag
Benha

Sîdi Abd el Rahman • Abusir
War Cemetery ■ • el Baramous • Bir Hooker
Álamein

Wadi el-Natrûn

el Qahira (CAIRO)
Pyramids & Sphinx ■
Memphis ■
Saqqâra ■
Birket Qarûn
Faiyûm Oasis • Da
el Faiyûm

Beni Suef

Maghâgha
Beni Mazâr

el Minya

Tuna el Gebel ■
Mallawi •
Dairût • T
Deir el Muharraq ■ • Ar
Manfalût

Asyû

Libyan Plateau

Qattâra Depression

■ Siwa Oasis
Siwa •

Bahariya Oasis
Bawiti •

White Desert

Qasr Farafra • *Farafra Oasis*

Western Desert

Libyan Desert

Dakhla Oasis
Mût • • el Qasr

el Khârga •

el Khârga Oasis

Bârîs •

465m ▲ *Abu Ballas*

Gilf Kebir Plateau

A   B   C (SD)

(L-R)

N (Nile)

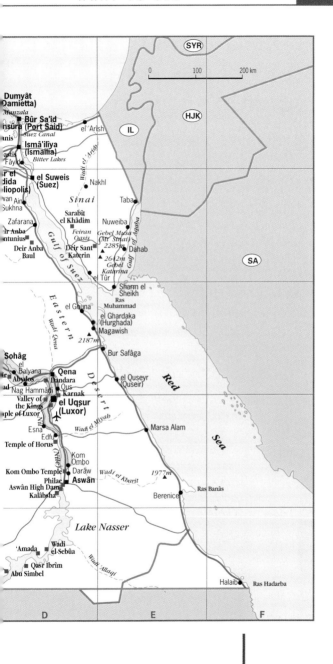

El-Qahira (Cairo) & Environs

Legendary King Menes founded his capital Memphis on the exact spot where the Delta met the Nile Valley. The modern day suburb of Matariya was the important ancient religious centre of On, while the Romans set up camp in Babylon, now known as Coptic Cairo. The city of el-Qahira or the Victorious (Cairo) was founded in AD 969 by the Fatimid Dynasty as a palace enclave. It soon grew into a great medieval city, enriched by the trade with the East and the West. Fatimid Cairo was centred around the el-Azhar Mosque, and enclosed within city walls which still exist in parts. The city soon burst out of its walls, and it has not stopped growing yet. In the mid-19th century Ismail Pasha created the European-style quarters on a flood plain, which now form downtown, and the city now spreads far into the desert on all sides.

> *'Travellers tell us that there is not on earth's face aught fairer than Cairo and her Nile...' Quoth my father, 'Whoso hath not seen Cairo hath not seen the world.'*

Tale of the Jewish Doctor, from the
Thousand and One Nights

Cairo

Cairo can be a challenging place to visit for the first time. Nearly 17 million people, several thousand years of history and a mixture of cultural influences from Africa, Asia and Europe add up to a serious assault on the senses. But Cairo somehow reconciles its extremes; great beauty with urban and industrial sprawl, affluence with poverty, the long shadow of the past with the promise of the future. Although it makes demands on its visitors (the traffic, pollution and hassles), its citizens make up for that by being some of the most hospitable and humorous people in the world.

Sultan Hassan and Rifai Mosques at Cairo

What to See in Cairo

AMR IBN EL-AS MOSQUE ⭐⭐

Amr, the Arab general who conquered Christian Egypt in AD 641, established the city of Fustat here, near the Roman fortress of Babylon. Fustat, famous for its ceramics and glassware, was a wealthy and sophisticated city until the 12th century. In 1168 it was burned to avoid it falling to the Crusaders – the fire lasted for 54 days – and has remained a mound of rubble ever since. Amr's Mosque, the first in Egypt, was later restored and underwent many more renovations, the last being in the 1970s. Look for the old features, particularly columns reused from churches and temples. In the far left corner lies Amr's son, Abdallah. Originally buried inside his house, his tomb was incorporated into the mosque during the 9th-century.

✚ 32B1
✉ 500m north of Mari Girgis, Coptic Cairo
🕐 Daily 9–4 (closed 12–1 Fri)
🚇 Mari Girgis
 Cheap
↔ El-Muallaqa church (➤ 40), Ben Ezra Synagogue (➤ 36), Coptic Museum (➤ 40)

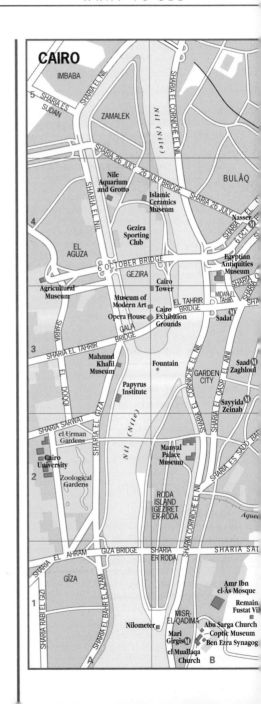

CAIRO

IMBABA

ZAMALEK

Nil (Nile)

SHARIA ES SUDAN

SHARIA EL NIL

SHARIA EL CORNICHE EL NIL

BULÂQ

SHARIA 26 JULY

26 JULY BRIDGE

SHARIA 26 JULY

Nile Aquarium and Grotto

Islamic Ceramics Museum

Nasser

Gezira Sporting Club

6 OCT

EL AGUZA

SHARIA EL NIL

6 OCTOBER BRIDGE

GEZIRA

Egyptian Antiquities Museum

Cairo Tower

SHARIA C

Agricultural Museum

SHARIA TAHRIR

Museum of Modern Art

Opera House

Cairo Exhibition Grounds

EL TAHRIR

MIDAN EL TAHIR

CAIRO BRIDGE

Sadat

SHA

GALA BRIDGE

SHARIA EL TAHRIR

EL DOQQI

Mahmud Khalil Museum

Fountain

SHARIA EL CORNICHE EL NIL

GARDEN CITY

SHARIA EL QASR EL AINI

Saad Zaghloul

Papyrus Institute

SHARIA SARWAT

el Urman Gardens

SHARIA EL GIZA

Nil (Nile)

Sayyida Zeinab

SHARIA ES SADD BA

Cairo University

Zoological Gardens

Manyal Palace Museum

RODA ISLAND (GEZIRET ER-RODA)

Aqued

SHARIA EL AHRAM

GIZA BRIDGE

SHARIA ER RODA

SHARIA CORNICHE EL NIL

SHARIA SAI

SHARIA RABI EL GIZI

SHARIA EL BAHR EL AZAM

GÎZA

Amr Ibn el-Âs Mosque

Remain Fustat Vil

MISR-EL-QADIMA

Nilometer

Mari Girgis

Abu Sarga Church

Coptic Museum

Ben Ezra Synagog

el Muallaqa Church

B

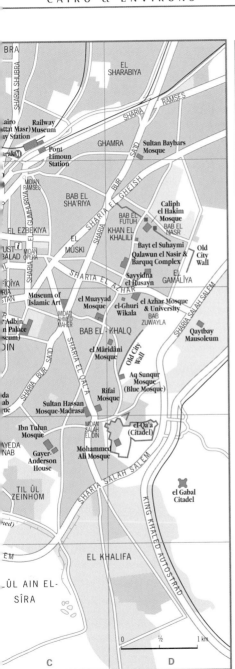

BRA

EL SHARABIYA

SHARIA SHUBRA

SHARIA RAMSES

SHARIA

airo
attat Masr) **Railway Museum**
ay Station

GHAMRA

SAID

Sultan Baybars Mosque

arak M

Pont Limoun Station

BUR

SHARIA EL GHEISH

MIDAN RAMSES

BAB EL SHA'RIYA

Caliph el Hakim Mosque

SHARIA GUMHURIYA

EL EZBEKIYA

SHARIA EL GUMHURIYA

BAB EL FUTUH

BAB EL NASR

EL MÛSKI

KHAN EL KHALILI

Bayt el Suhaymi

Old City Wall

UST
BALAD

MIDAN OPERA

Qalawun el Nasir & Barquq Complex

EL GAMALÎYA

ÎQÎYA

RIA
TAN

Sayyidna el Husayn

SHARIA EL AZHAR

Museum of Islamic Art

el Muayyad Mosque

el-Ghuri Wikala

el Azhar Mosque & University

SHARIA SALAH SALEM

Adbin
n Palace
seum)
DIN

MIDAN AHMED MAHER

BAB EL KHALQ

BAB ZUWAYLA

Qaytbay Mausoleum

SHARIA BUR SAID

SHARIA EL QAL'A

el Mâridâni Mosque

Old City Wall

da
ab
ue

Rifai Mosque

Aq Sunqur Mosque (Blue Mosque)

Ibn Tulun Mosque

Sultan Hassan Mosque-Madrasa

MIDAN SALAH EL DIN

el-Qa'a (Citadel)

AYEDA
NAB

Gayer-Anderson House

Mohammed Ali Mosque

TIL ÛL ZEINHOM

SHARIA SALAH SALEM

el Gabal Citadel

KING KHALED AUTOSTRAD

ned)

EM

EL KHALIFA

ÛL AIN EL-SÎRA

0   ½   1 km

C   D

✚ 33D3

✉ Sharia el-Azhar, Midan el-Husayn

🕐 Daily 8–7 (closed 11–1 Fri)

✋ Moderate

↔ Sayyidna el-Husayn (➤ 43), Khan el-Khalili (➤ 22), Wikala el-Ghuri (➤ 43), Bab Zuwayla (➤ below), Museum of Islamic Art (➤ 38)

❓ Dress modestly, cover arms and legs

EL-AZHAR MOSQUE AND UNIVERSITY ✪✪

El-Azhar ('the most blooming'), founded in AD 971, was the first mosque in the Fatimid city, and claims to be the oldest university in the world. As Egypt's supreme theological authority, the Sheikh of el-Azhar plays a significant role in national politics. The mosque is entered through the remarkable 18th-century Barber's Gate, where students traditionally had their heads shaved. Beyond is a large *sahn* or courtyard, part of the original 10th-century design, overlooked by three minarets. To the right is a Mameluke *madrasa* (Quranic school), with apartments for Quranic students. The oldest part of the building is the east *liwan* (hall), in which many ancient alabaster pillars were reused. The university now occupies several large modern blocks behind the mosque.

✚ 33D3

✉ Bab Zuwayla is in Darb el-Ahmar. Bab el-Futuh and Bab el-Nasr are on the other end of Sharia el-Muizz lidin Allah

🕐 Look for the custodian around Bab el-Futuh who will let you into the gates

✋ Cheap

↔ Bayt el-Suhaymi (➤ 36), Khan el-Khalili (➤ 22), El-Azhar Mosque (➤ above), also walk ➤ 35

BAB ZUWAYLA AND OTHER CITY GATES ✪✪

Bab Zuwayla, built in 1092 and also known as Bab el-Mitwalli, was the southern gate of the Fatimid city. From the terrace between its imposing twin towers, Mameluke sultans watched the departure of the annual caravan of pilgrims to Mecca. A small museum inside the restored gatehouse illustrates the history of the gate and also explains about the 19th-century saint Mitwalli el-Qutb who performed miracles here. Adjacent to the gates is the 15th-century el-Muayyad Mosque with a tree-shaded courtyard. On the northern side of the Fatimid city are the Bab el-Futuh (Gate of Conquests) and Bab el-Nasr (Gate of Victory), joined by a 200m-long tunnel with fine brick work.

DID YOU KNOW?

Next to Bab el-Futuh is the 11th-century mosque of the strange blue-eyed Caliph, el-Hakim. As he loved night-time, he decreed that this would be the time for work while the days were for sleeping. He hated women so much they were not allowed to go out and women's cobblers were closed down. He also had all Cairo's dogs killed for making too much noise. After his death, the Druze (a heretical Muslim sect) proclaimed that he would return as the Messiah.

Above: for more than 1,000 years el-Azhar has offered free education and board to students from all over the Islamic world

Walk between Two City Gates

Start at the beautifully restored Bab Zuwayla (➤ 34) and walk along Sharia el-Muizz lidin Allah.

Find the small entrance on the inside of the Bab Zuwayla Gate and climb up the minaret for spectacular views over the city.

Back on the street, turn left and continue past a little square where cotton is sold, with the 19th-century Sabil of Muhammad Ali. A hundred metres on stands the ruined 12th-century Fakahani Mosque. Fifty metres further, on the left, are the city's last two tarboush (fez) shops.

Just before the intersection with Sharia el-Azhar is the Ghuriya complex, with the splendid 16th-century Mosque-Madrasa of el-Ghuri (left) and the Mausoleum of el-Ghuri and the el-Ghuri Palace (right), now under restoration (➤ 113).

Cross via the walking bridge and continue along the more touristy end of Sharia el-Muizz.

After 50m, around the Madrasa of Barsbey, shops sell spices, perfume, fetishes and herbal remedies. After the intersection with El-Muski, the street turns into the Gold Bazaar and further on into the Coppersmiths' Bazaar. Past this to the right is the Madrasa of Sultan Ayyub and to the left the superb Qalawun, el-Nasir and Barquq complex (➤ 41).

With Qasr Bashtak on the right, take the left-hand fork at the lovely drinking fountain Sabil-Kuttab of Katkhuda. One block past the 12th-century Mosque of el-Aqmar, 70m further to the right, turn right into Darb el-Asfar for Bayt el-Suhaymi (➤ 36). Return to the main street and turn right, past the El-Silahdar Mosque. Continue through the lemon and garlic market to the Mosque of el-Hakim, built against the Northern Walls and the Bab el-Futuh (➤ 34).

Distance
1½km

Time
Half an hour without stops, at least half day with stops

Start point
Bab Zuwayla
➕ 33D3

End point
Bab el-Futuh
➕ 33D4

The courtyard of the el-Muayyad Mosque offers a peaceful retreat from the bustle of the souks

35

✠ 33C2

✉ 4 Midan Ahmed ibn
Tulun, Sayyida Zaynab

☎ 02-364 7822

🕐 Daily 8–4. Closed 12–1 Fri

🚌 174; minibus No 54 from
bus station behind the
Egyptian Museum

💷 Moderate

↔ Ibn Tulun Mosque
(➤ 37), Citadel (➤ 41),
Sultan Hassan Mosque-
Madrasa (➤ 26)

✠ 33D4

✉ 19 Darb el-Asfar, el-
Gamaliya

🕐 Daily 9–5

🚌 66

💷 Moderate

↔ Bab el-Futuh (➤ 34),
Qalawun complex
(➤ 41), Khan el-Khalili
(➤ 22)

---

*The synagogue was also
used for keeping valuable
sacred documents which
included one of the oldest
known Torahs in the
world*

✠ 32B1

✉ Mari Girgis, Coptic Cairo

🕐 Daily 8–4

🚇 Mari Girgis

♿ Few

💷 Free, donations welcome

↔ El-Muallaqa (➤ 40),
Coptic Museum (➤ 40)

BAYT EL-KRITILIYA (GAYER-ANDERSON HOUSE) ✪✪

The Gayer-Anderson House, two adjoining 16th- and 17th-century mansions, is an orientalist's dream. The orientalist in question was a British major, R J Gayer-Anderson, who lived here from 1935 to 1942 and collected ancient Egyptian and Oriental art. The spacious and harmoniously decorated *qa'a* (men's reception room) appeared in the 1977 James Bond film *The Spy Who Loved Me*, and is one of the finest such rooms in Cairo. The *harem* (women's and children's quarters) includes a succession of finely decorated rooms, a roof terrace to take the air and secret windows which allowed the women to look onto the *qa'a* without being seen.

BAYT EL-SUHAYMI ✪✪

This remarkable 16th- and 17th-century house, which belonged to a wealthy merchant and his many wives and concubines, is a labyrinth of rooms for the men followed by rooms for the *harem* (women and children). They are all beautifully decorated and perfectly air-conditioned in traditional style, centred around a cool, peaceful courtyard where it is pleasant to linger for a while.

BEN EZRA SYNAGOGUE ✪✪

The splendidly restored Ben Ezra Synagogue is the oldest surviving synagogue in Egypt. Formerly the 4th-century Church of St Michael, it is built in basilica style with three naves and a hidden altar, and the intricate decoration is not unlike that of the nearby churches. Copts believe that this was where Moses was found in a basket, while Jews claim that Jeremiah preached here in the 6th century. Services are no longer held.

GEZIRA ✪✪

Gezira, the largest island on the Nile in Cairo, is crossed by three bridges. The exclusive residential area Zamalek, on the northern side, has many up-market shops and restaurants and is home to the Gezira Sporting Club (➤ 115), founded in 1877 by the British Army. Near the Marriott Hotel, a former palace, is the Gezira Centre of Arts with a museum of Islamic Ceramics (➤ 38). The landmarks on the Gezira (southern) end are the Cairo Tower and the Opera House. The 187m-high Cairo Tower, built in the late 1950s, has a revolving restaurant and, on a clear day, sweeping views over Cairo to the desert. The Opera House (➤ 113), a gift from Japan, was built in 1988 to replace the one that burned down in 1971. In its grounds is the Museum of Egyptian Modern Art and several galleries.

➕ 32A4
✉ Gezira Island
🕐 Cairo Tower daily 9AM–midnight; Modern Art Museum closed for restoration
🍴 Café/restaurant on top of Cairo Tower (££)
🚇 Gezira
🚌 Minibus 54
♿ Few
💷 Cairo Tower moderate, museums cheap

IBN TULUN MOSQUE ✪✪✪

Built by Ahmed Ibn Tulun in AD 876–9, this exquisite mosque is a rare example of the classical period in Islamic architecture (9th to 10th centuries). The peaceful courtyard, with its simple grandeur, was built as a vast, open-air prayer hall – this was the city's central mosque and is now its oldest intact Islamic monument. The 2km-long sycamore-wood frieze is said to contain one-fifth of the Koran in Kufic inscriptions. The unusual minaret with an outside spiral staircase was inspired by the architecture of Samarra in Iraq, where Tulun grew up, although local lore has it that the sultan absent-mindedly rolled up a piece of paper and handed it to the architect as being the design.

➕ 33C2
✉ Midan Ahmed Ibn Tulun
🕐 Daily 8–6
♿ Few
💷 Cheap
↔ Gayer-Anderson House (➤ 36), Citadel (➤ 41), Sultan Hassan Mosque-Madrasa (➤ 26)

KHAN EL-KHALILI (➤ 22, TOP TEN)

Above: *The boldly designed Opera House, a combination of Oriental and Western styles on the island of Gezira in Cairo*

37

+ 33C3
✉ Sharia Bur Said on intersection with Sharia el Qal'a
☎ 02-390 9930
◔ Sat–Thu 9–4, Fri 9–11:30, 1–4
♿ Few
▥ Moderate
↔ Bab Zuwayla (► 34), Tentmakers' Bazaar (► 107)
? The museum is undergoing extensive renovation and reorganisation and is due to reopen in spring 2005.

EL-MATHAF EL-ISLAMI (MUSEUM OF ISLAMIC ART) ✪✪

This rare and extensive collection of Islamic arts holds the key to understanding the architecture of Islamic Cairo. Seeing the appalling state of many Cairene mosques and palaces, Khedive Tewfiq founded a museum of Islamic art in 1880 to salvage parts of derelict buildings. All exhibits are arranged chronologically or by medium, and are dated AH – *anno hegirae*, the Year of the Hegira, when Muhammad fled from Mecca to Medina, which is the beginning of the Islamic Calendar (AD 622). Sunni Muslims consider the representation of human and animal figures as idolatry, so there are no statues in the museum and most of the exhibits are based on floral motifs, geometric patterns and Arabic calligraphy. The exception to this rule was the art of the Shi'a Fatimids who allowed birds, animals and scenes from daily life in the decoration of their objects. Amongst the masterpieces are the amazing door from Sayyida Zaynab's mosque, a 14th-century Mameluke fountain and fine glass lamps. (► side panel.)

+ 32A4
✉ Gezira Art Centre, 1 Sharia el-Marsafy, Zamalek
☎ 02-736 8672
◔ Sat–Thu 9–1
♿ Few
▥ Free
? Complex includes several art galleries, an open-air theatre and a cinema

MATHAF EL-KHAZAF EL-ISLAMI (ISLAMIC CERAMICS MUSEUM) ✪✪

The domed palace of Prince Amr Ibrahim, a neo-Islamic, 20th-century building, houses a wonderful range of ceramics from all over the Islamic world, put together from the collections of the Egyptian royal family, Prince Amr Ibrahim and the Museum of Islamic Art (see above). The well-displayed collection has several rare pieces, including a precious 17th-century porcelain plate from Andalucia and a very fine 16th-century Turkish *mishkaa* or hanging lamp.

EL-MATHAF EL-MASRI (EGYPTIAN MUSEUM) (► 23, TOP TEN)

Intricate geometrical screens decorate the sumptuous interior of the early 20th-century Manyal Palace

Detail of a carved clock tower with Arabic numerals on the clock face, one of the treasures of the Manyal Palace Museum

MATHAF MAHMUD KHALIL
(MAHMUD KHALIL MUSEUM)

This splendid little museum is home to a superb collection of original French impressionist paintings and fine sculpture, which comes as something of a surprise to tourists, very few of whom visit the place. Little known paintings by the likes of Renoir, Monet, Van Gogh, Pissarro, Gauguin and Ingres, sculptures by artists such as Rodin, as well as Chinese porcelain and jade, were lovingly gathered by Mahmud Khalil, a pre-war agricultural minister, and his French wife. They bequeathed their collection to the state on the condition that it would be displayed in their own Italianate villa and the air-conditioned rooms offer welcome relief on a hot summer's day.

- ✚ 32A3
- ✉ 1 Sharia Kafour, Giza, next to the Maglis el-Dawla (State Council)
- ☎ 02-336 2358
- 🕐 Tue–Sun 10–5:30. Closed Mon
- ♿ Very good
- 💵 Moderate
- ↔ Gezira (► 37)
- ❓ You need your ID or passport to enter the museum

MATHAF QASR EL-MANYAL
(MANYAL PALACE MUSEUM)

Built in an amazing cocktail of architectural styles, from Persian and Moorish to Ottoman and Rococo, this early 20th-century palace belonged to King Farouk's uncle, Prince Muhammad Ali. The Reception Palace is finely decorated with stained glass and colourful tiles, and of the series of rooms upstairs the Syrian Room is the finest, with exquisite inlay of mother-of-pearl. Most rooms in the Royal Residence have wonderful blue tiling, while the Private Museum houses an interesting collection of porcelain, pictures, rugs and copies of the Koran. A bizarre display of dusty and ragged stuffed animals is on show in the Trophies Museum, near the gate. The once magnificent gardens are being restored to their former glory.

- ✚ 32B2
- ✉ Near el-Gamaa Bridge, Roda Island
- ☎ 02-368 7495
- 🕐 Daily 9–5
- ♿ Few
- 💵 Moderate

39

✠ 32B1
✉ Coptic Cairo
☎ 02-363 9742
🕐 Daily 9–4 (closed Fri 11–1)
🍴 Café in the garden (£)
Ⓜ Mari Girgis
✋ Moderate
↔ El-Muallaqa (➤ below), Ben Ezra Synagogue (➤ 36)
❓ The museum is undergoing extensive renovation and is due to reopen in spring 2005.

Below: *Coptic papyri illustrate how the Copts followed ancient Egyptian techniques and traditions*

EL-MATHAF EL-QIBTI (COPTIC MUSEUM) ✪✪✪

The Coptic Museum's valuable collection of secular and religious Coptic artefacts, from AD 200–1800, shows fascinating evidence of ancient Egyptian influence on early Christianity. The ground floor of the New Wing is arranged chronologically, starting with early Christian reliefs suggesting that the Christian cross developed from the pharaonic *ankh* (the 'key of life' looped cross). Note also the wonderful frescoes from the 6th-century el-Bawit monastery. Room 6 has the earliest recorded stone pulpit from the 6th-century St Jeremiah monastery in Saqqara, while Room 10 claims to have the oldest surviving book in the world, a 1,600-year-old copy of the Psalms of David. Some magnificent Coptic textiles are on display on the upper floor. The Old Wing, remarkable in itself for the fine woodwork and ceiling carvings, houses some interesting pottery and artefacts from Coptic churches. The towers and walls in the garden were built by Roman Emperor Trajan around AD 130 as part of Babylon. (➤ side panel.)

✠ 32B1
✉ Coptic Cairo
🕐 Mon–Sat 9–5, Sun 12–5
Ⓜ Mari Girgis
♿ Few
✋ Free; donations welcome. Well-informed Coptic students often guide visitors round
↔ Coptic Museum (➤ above), Ben Ezra Synagogue (➤ 36)

EL-MUALLAQA (HANGING CHURCH) ✪✪✪

The Hanging Church, built over a Roman Gate, is reached via an impressive stairway, which leads to a vestibule where videos of papal sermons and wonderfully kitsch Coptic shrines are on sale. Copts believe that the church was founded in the 4th century, but it could date to at least 300 years after that. The main nave, with a ceiling vaulted like an ark, is separated from the aisles by 16 pillars that probably carried images of saints. The altar areas are hidden by finely carved wooden screens inlaid with ivory and the exquisite marble pulpit is supported by 12 pillars, one for each of the apostles.

EL-QAL'A (CITADEL) ✪✪✪

Realising the difficulty of protecting Cairo, Salah el-Din el-Ayyubi (Saladin) built the Citadel in the 12th century. Its design was strongly influenced by Crusader castles in Palestine and Syria. The most obvious building, seen from many parts of Cairo, is the 19th-century Mosque of Muhammad Ali, inspired by grand Ottoman mosques in Istanbul. Inside, despite the soaring dome, the lack of proportion and the overdone decor are disappointing. The courtyard clock was a gift from King Louis-Philippe of France, in exchange for the Luxor obelisk now in the Place de la Concorde, Paris. Next door is the 14th-century Mosque of el-Nasir with a tiled minaret, and the Gawhara Palace, the former royal quarters, built in a French style. Among several museums, there is the Carriage Museum, the National Police Museum and the Seized Museum.

✚ 33D2
⊠ Entrance at Bab al-Gabal, on the Salah Salem road
🕐 Daily 8–6 summer, 8–5 winter. Museums close 4:30
🍴 Café (£)   🚌 Bus 82
♿ Few
💷 Moderate
↔ Sultan Hasan Mosque-Madrasa (➤ 26), Ibn Tulun Mosque (➤ 37), Bab Zuwayla (➤ 34)

Above: *the Mosque of Muhammad Ali in the Citadel*

QALAWUN, EL-NASIR AND BARQUQ COMPLEX ✪✪✪

The splendid 185m-long façade of this Mameluke complex is one of Cairo's most wonderful sights. Coming from el-Azhar, the first building is Qalawun's *maristan* (hospital and madhouse) built in 1285 and used as such until 1850. Next door is the beautifully restored and richly decorated mausoleum of Sultan Qalawun and behind it a *madrasa* (Koranic school). His son el-Nasir Muhammad, who is also buried in this mausoleum, followed his father's plan and in 1304 built a mosque, a *madrasa* and mausoleum next door. Barquq, the first Circassian Mameluke sultan, added his share to it and in 1386 built a fine *khanqah* (religious hostel) and a magnificent *madrasa* behind heavy bronze-plated doors with silver inlay.

✚ 33D4
⊠ Bayn el-Qasrayn, Sharia Muzz lidin Allah
🕐 Daily 8–5
💷 Cheap (plus tips)
↔ Bayt el-Suhaymi (➤ 36), Khan el-Khalili (➤ 22), Sayyidna el-Husayn Mosque (➤ 43), Bab el-Futuh (➤ 34)
❓ The complex is undergoing restoration

33C3
Midan Abdin, Downtown
02-391 0042
Sat–Thu 9–3
Mohamed Naguib
Few
Moderate
Wust el-Balad (see opposite), Museum of Islamic Art (▶ 38)
No cameras

QASR ABDIN (ABDIN PALACE MUSEUM) ✪✪

Khedive Ismail built this 500-room palace as part of the redevelopment of Cairo to accompany the opening of the Suez Canal in 1869. Four years later he moved the royal family here from the Citadel, where they lived until the revolution in 1952 (fulfilling a prophecy that the dynasty would only survive if it stayed in the Citadel). The main palace is closed to the public, but in a separate building there are displays of weaponry and suits of armour, as well as part of the former royal family's impressive collection of silver, china and crystal. The medal museum contains King Farouk's amusing collection of badges.

33D3
El-Qarafa el-Sharqiya (Northern Cemetery), el-Dirasa
Daily 9–8
Minibus No 77
Free

QAYTBAY MAUSOLEUM-MADRASA ✪✪✪

The grandest building in the Northern Cemetery belonged to the last powerful Mameluke ruler, Sultan Qaytbay, who reigned from 1468 to 1496. This jewel of late Mameluke architecture is perfect in many ways, with faultless proportions, fine carving around the doors and windows and an elegant minaret. Although the decoration of the *madrasa* (Koranic school) is amazingly rich, the overall effect is one of simplicity and harmony, using the primary Islamic designs: calligraphy, arabesque and geometric patterns. The tomb chamber, one of the most impressive in Cairo, is covered by a magnificent huge dome.

The perfectly proportioned dome of Qaytbay's mausoleum is decorated with fine polygonal reliefs

The modern mosque of Sayyidna el-Husayn with its Turkish-style minarets was built over an earlier Fatimid mosque

SAYYIDNA EL-HUSAYN MOSQUE ✪

One of Cairo's most sacred mosques dedicated to the Prophet Muhammad's grandson Husayn, who was killed in 680 in Iraq. Although it has been disputed that his head is buried here, Husayn has emerged as the city's patron saint and his mosque attracts Muslims from around the world, particularly during the annual *moulid* (birthday celebration). Cairenes believe the whole area, including the cafés, around the mosque has a special *baraka* (blessing) and so it is a popular place in the evening. Alcohol is forbidden.

SULTAN HASAN MOSQUE-MADRASA
(► 26, TOP TEN)

WIKALAT EL-GHURI ✪✪

This restored Mameluke caravanserai (merchants' inn and storehouse) is an oasis of cool, calm and silence amidst the hubbub of the bazaars and lively streets of the old city. It now provides workshops for craftsmen and studios for painters, some of which can be visited. Traditional crafts are on sale. The 16th-century courtyard is used for theatre and concerts and houses an exhibition of peasant and bedouin crafts.

WUST EL-BALAD (DOWNTOWN) ✪✪

The reconstruction of central Cairo was another of Khedive Ismail's extravagant projects for the inauguration of the Suez Canal in 1869. Impressed with Paris's boulevards, he built elegant avenues like Talaat Harb and Qasr el-Nil. Nowadays the streets are congested and many buildings have been demolished, but a walk downtown still has its rewards, particularly when you look up at the grand 19th-century colonial-style buildings. Midan el-Tahrir, Cairo's main square, and the Nile Hilton complex were created after the 1952 revolution on the site of the British barracks.

🚩 33D4
✉ Midan el-Husayn
💷 Free
↔ El-Azhar Mosque (► 34), Khan el-Khalili (► 22), Wikalat el-Ghuri (► below)
❓ Closed to non-Muslims. *The* place to be or to avoid during major Muslim festivals

---

🚩 33D3
✉ Off Sharia Muizz lidin Allah, near el-Azhar Mosque
🕐 Daily 9–5. Closed Fri
💷 Cheap
↔ El-Azhar Mosque (► 34), Khan el-Khalili (► 22)

🚩 33C4
🕐 Most shops are closed Sun
🍴 Cafés and restaurants (£–£££)
🚇 Sadat
♿ Few
↔ Egyptian Museum (► 23)

In the Know

If you only have a short time to visit Egypt and would like to get a real flavour of the country, here are some ideas:

10
Ways to Be a Local

- **Always take time for extensive greetings**: *salaam alaykum*, *sabah el-ward* (a morning full of roses), *sabah el-yasmin* (a morning of jasmine).
- **Take your time**, and try to use the expressions *inshallah* (if God wills), *bukra* (tomorrow) and *ma'alesh* (never mind) as often as you can.
- **Eat *fuul*** (stewed fava beans) for breakfast.
- **Take your shoes off** when visiting mosques.
- **Watch a belly dance** show at 3AM rather than the tourist version at 8PM.
- **Have a joke** or humorous remark for every occasion.
- **Sit on a café terrace** and smoke a *sheesha* (waterpipe).
- **Cheer loudly** at actors when watching a film in the cinema.
- **Stare in amazement** at fine ancient carvings in tombs and temples.
- **Take to the river** after a hot day, and watch the sun go down from a slow-sailing felucca.

Lose yourself watching the water bubble at the bottom of a pipe and then inhale its honey-sweetened smoke

10
Good Places to Have Lunch

- **Al-Moudira (££–£££)**, Daba'iyya, West Bank Luxor ☎ 012-325 1307. Delightful salads and Lebanese dishes poolside.
- **Andrea (£–££)**, 59-60 Marioutiya Canal, el-Ahram, Giza ☎ 02-383 1133. Succulent roast chicken in a peaceful garden (➤ 92).
- **Arabica (£–££)**, 13 Sharia Ahmed Hishmet, Zamalek ☎ 02-735 7982. Excellent *fateer* (Egyptian pizzas).
- **Aswan Moon (££)**, Corniche an-Nil, Aswan ☎ 316 108. Fresh juices, Nubian stews and salads while watching the river flow past (➤ 92).
- **Felfela Garden (£–££)**, 15 Sharia Hoda Shaarawi, Downtown Cairo ☎ 02-392 2833. For *mezze* and stuffed pigeon (➤ 92–93).
- **Fish Market (££–£££)**, 26 Corniche el-Nil, Alexandria ☎ 03-480 5114. Superb fish. Great views (➤ 95).
- **Kenooz (£-££)**, Sharia Subukha, Siwa Town ☎ 046-460 1299. Delicious vegetable stews in the shade of palm trees (➤ 97).
- **Marriott Garden (£)**, Marriott Hotel, Zamalek, Cairo ☎ 02-735 8888. Club sandwiches, grills and pizzas in a palace garden (➤ 100).
- **Naguib Mahfouz Coffee Shop (£)**, 5 el-Bedestan alley, Khan el-Khalili, Cairo

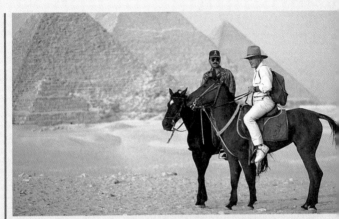

Riding round the pyramids is an exhilarating excursion but very tiring

☎ 02-590 3788. Watch the crowds in the bazaar (➤ 93).
• **Restaurant Mohammed (£-££)**, Gurna, West Bank Luxor ☎ 095-311 014. Excellent Egyptian basics prepared with love (➤ 97).

10
Top Activities

• **Birdwatching** at Wadi Rayan in Faiyum (➤ 46).
• **Desert driving** in the Western Desert (➤ 114).
• **Diving** in the Red Sea (➤ 89).
• **Felucca sailing** between Aswan and Luxor (➤ 78).
• **Hot air ballooning** over Luxor with Balloons over Egypt (☎ 095-376516).
• **Swimming** Most luxury hotels allow non-residents to use their pool for a fee.
• **Windsurfing** in the Red Sea, especially Moon Beach Resort, Ras Sudr (☎ 069-401500)

• **Hiking** in Sinai (information from St Catherine's Protectorate ☎ 062-470 032).
• **Horse riding** at the Pyramids of Giza or on the West Bank in Luxor (stables ➤ 115)
• **Fishing** safaris on Lake Nasser (for information ☎ 097-316 052)

5
Best Markets

• **El-Muski** in Cairo. Busy street market with toys, textiles, stationery, clothes and household goods, Mon–Sat.
• **Souk el-Gimal** in Birqash, 30km northwest of Cairo, early on Monday and Friday mornings. Camels from Sudan are sold, plus goats and saddles.
• **Souk el-Gimal** in Daraw. Sudanese traders sell their camels to local farmers in this colourful market (➤ 80).
• **Tewfiqiya Market**, Downtown, Cairo.

Excellent food and vegetable market.
• **Sharia el-Suq**, Aswan. Laid back market full of fetishes, lovely baskets, silk shawls and stuffed baby crocodiles.

5
Best Views

• Sunset over Islamic and modern Cairo, and the pyramids from the terrace of the Muhammad Ali Mosque (➤ 41).
• Climb the path above Deir el-Bahri (➤ 70) for views over the mortuary temples, fluorescent green sugarcane fields and the Nile in Luxor.
• Feluccas catching the wind and Aswan in the background from the Aga Khan Mausoleum (➤ 76)
• Take a room in the Cecil Hotel (➤ 102) with sweeping views over the Corniche in Alexandria.
• See the sun rise over Sinai from the summit of Gebel Musa in St Catherine's Protectorate (➤ 19).

45

What to See Around Cairo

EL-AHRAM AND ABU'L HOL (PYRAMIDS AND SPHINX)
(► 17, TOP TEN)

DAHSHUR ✪✪

Wealthy Cairenes choose the quiet countryside of Dahshur to build their weekend retreats, but it also has two impressive Old Kingdom pyramids, both built by Snefru (c2613–1588 BC), the father of Khufu, which give an insight into the evolution of pyramid building. The imposing Bent Pyramid, its shiny white limestone casing intact in places, is unlike any other pyramid. It rises more steeply than the pyramid of Khufu but suddenly changes to a gentler angle near the top. The Red Pyramid, its sides built at a 43-degree angle, is considered the first 'true' pyramid.

✚ 28C4
✉ 5km south of Saqqara
◷ Daily 8–5
Moderate
↔ Saqqara (► 48–9), Memphis (► 47)

EL-FAIYUM ✪✪

Faiyum is surrounded by desert but is not a real oasis as it is connected to the Nile via the Bahr Yusuf. Faiyum town is a dull provincial centre, most famous for its water-wheels, particularly the Seven Waterwheels north of town. Its main attractions lie in its environs, especially Birket Qarun, a salt lake which attracts Cairenes for a rowing session and hunters looking for duck and geese. The waterfalls and freshwater lakes of Wadi Rayan, near the village of Tunis, are an ideal place to swim and watch birds. There are several ancient sites in the area, including the well-preserved Ptolemaic temple of Qasr Qarun, the ruins of a Ptolemaic-Roman town at Kom Aushim (just off the Cairo road) and the Pyramid of Meidoum.

✚ 28C4
✉ 100km southwest of Cairo
ℹ Midan Qarun, next to the waterwheels
🍴 Café (£–££) and restaurant on the lake (££)
🚌 Frequent buses from Cairo under the Munib Bridge in Giza

Opposite: *Birket Qarun no longer has the crocodiles worshipped by the Graeco-Romans, but there is still plenty of fish and fowl*

Left: *solar boats were probably used in Khufu's funerary procession and then buried to be used in the Underworld*

MATHAF MARKIB EL-SHAMS (SOLAR BOAT MUSEUM)

✪✪✪

Five boat pits were discovered at the foot of the Pyramid of Khufu (► 17) and the 43m-long boat in the Solar Boat Museum was found in one of them. The boat, made of cedarwood, was in thousands of pieces, which took restorer Hagg Ahmed Yusuf fourteen years and a lot of patience to reconstruct. The result was worth it, for this simple boat is one of the most attractive of all Egyptian antiquities. Another boat, discovered in perfect condition in 1987, was left buried in the sand. The purpose of these boats remains unclear.

➕ 28C4
✉ Giza Plateau, 18km southwest of Cairo
🕐 Daily 9–4 (5 in summer)
🚌 Minibus 83
♿ Moderate
↔ Giza Pyramids and Sphinx (► 17)

MEMPHIS

✪✪

Little remains of the world's first imperial capital beyond a few statues and columns. King Menes is said to have united Egypt's southern valley and northern delta around 3100 BC and then created a new capital at Memphis, symbolically placed where delta and valley meet. Memphis became a magnificent city and for thousands of years was either Egypt's capital or second city. Most buildings in Memphis were constructed using mudbrick and have long since disappeared. The stone-built ones fared no better as they were quarried over the centuries to provide materials for monuments elsewhere. A small New Kingdom sphinx and a limestone colossus of Ramses II as a young man are on show in a modern pavilion in the open-air museum.

➕ 28C4
✉ Mit Rahina, 24km south of Cairo
🕐 Daily 8–5
♿ Few
🏛 Moderate
↔ Saqqara (► 48–49)
❓ Public transport is difficult and it may be advisable to book a day trip to Memphis and Saqqara through a travel agent

47

🚩 29D4

✉ 5km north of centre of Cairo

🚇 Saray el-Qubba

🍴 Restaurants (££)

Below: *ancient Egyptians made pilgrimages to the Step Pyramid and considered its architect, Imhotep, a god*

🚩 28C4

✉ 2km west of Memphis

🕐 Daily 9–4

🍴 Café (£–££)

🚌 121 bus from Giza Pyramids to Badrasheen, then minibus to Saqqara village

♿ Moderate

↔ Memphis (➤ 47), Dahshur (➤ 46)

❓ The Step Pyramid can only be entered by special permit from the Egyptian Antiquities Inspectorate

---

MISR EL-GADIDA (HELIOPOLIS)   ✪

The city of the sun (On), which the Greeks called Heliopolis, was one of ancient Egypt's most important cult centres dedicated to the sun god Ra. Little has survived of the city beyond an obelisk raised by Pharaoh Senusert I, in nearby Matariya, but the modern suburb of Heliopolis is now a booming district. It was planned at the end of the 19th century by Belgian-born Baron Empain as a garden city. Empain's eccentric villa, built like a Cambodian temple, is now empty, but many grand villas and Moorish-style buildings along the elegant avenues are occupied, a testament to his vision. Amongst them, the former Heliopolis Palace Hotel is now the official presidency.

SAQQARA   ✪✪✪

Saqqara, the necropolis of the city of Memphis, is one of the largest (7km long and 1.5km wide) and most important cemeteries in Egypt, where much remains unexcavated. The Old Kingdom royal family and nobles were buried here, and the cemetery was in use for more than 3,000 years. The Step Pyramid of King Djoser, part of the largest funerary complex in Saqqara, was built by Djoser's architect, Imhotep, in the 27th century BC. It was both the first pyramid in Egypt and at that time the largest monument in the world built of hewn stone. The genius of Imhotep, who was later deified for his efforts, was that he started building a traditional *mastaba* (structure above tombs) not in mudbrick but in stone, and then added several more to create the six-step pyramid.

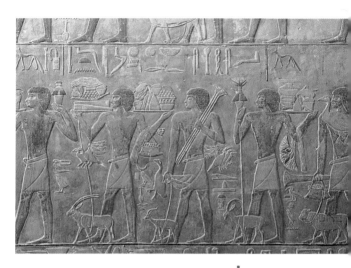

Visitors enter the funerary complex, originally enclosed by a limestone wall, from the rebuilt southeastern gate which leads to a Hypostyle Hall, and further on to the Great South Court. On the northern side of the pyramid stands the *serdab*, a box containing a replica of Djoser's life-size statue staring towards his immortality. Further northeast, next to the Pyramid of Teti, are two magnificent 6th-Dynasty *mastabas* of the Viziers Mereruka and Kagemni with the finest reliefs of the Old Kingdom. Next door, the *mastaba* of Ankh-ma-hor has particularly fine reliefs of craftsmen, and further west the *mastaba* of the Royal Hairdresser Ti has scenes from children's games. The Serapeum, the catacomb for the mummies of the sacred Apis bulls is now closed to the public. Walking back from the Serapeum towards the Step Pyramid, look for the *mastaba* of Akhti-Hotep and Ptah-Hotep which shows the various stages of the decoration of a tomb. South of Djoser's complex, the Pyramid of Unas contains a passageway leading to the burial chamber whose walls are decorated with the Pyramid texts, which are the earliest known example of decorative writing in a pharaonic tomb. The well-preserved *mastaba* of Queen Nebet, Unas's wife, has beautiful wall-paintings of the queen in the *harem* rooms of the palace, while the *mastaba* of Princess Idout gives an insight into the daily life of an Egyptian princess. Eastwards, the *mastaba* of Merou has splendid, very colourful scenes on the wall.

Exquisite wall carvings in the tomb of the priest Ptah-Hotep show a variety of offerings

Alexandria, the Northwest & the Oases

Alexandria was planned as Egypt's link to the Mediterranean world, but since many of its foreign residents left in the 1950s and 60s, the city has become increasingly conservative and Egyptian. Both Mersa Matruh, a trading post where Greeks traded with the northern Bedouin, and Rashid (Rosetta) popular with foreigners in the mid-19th century, are now also resolutely Egyptian towns.

The Western oases and particularly Siwa have a very distinct character, cut off as they are from the Nile Valley and the coast. Surrounded by the huge expanses of desert, and until last century, visited regularly only by camel caravans, their main income still comes from the palm groves and olive trees. Change is coming fast though with the Egyptian government's interest in resettling people from the Nile Valley, as well as the growth of desert tourism.

> *' There is not much to see here, nothing but the perpetual feeling of being in the East, the eastern colouring, the eastern atmosphere. '*
>
> FLORENCE NIGHTINGALE
> from *Letters from Egypt*
> 19 November 1849

Wall-paintings evoking a pilgrimage to Mecca

Alexandria

Alexandria, Egypt's second largest city, was famous throughout the classical world as a place of learning and of academic achievement – its icon was the Pharos, a lighthouse, one of the seven wonders of the world. Centuries after its heyday, when conquered by the Arabs in AD 641, it was still described as a marble city of 4,000 palaces and 400 theatres.

Little beyond fragments of ancient Alexandria is visible in the city, but exciting finds have been made in the Eastern harbour including remains of Cleopatra's Palace and the Pharos. The new Bibliotheca Alexandrina pays tribute to the famous ancient library, the Mouseion, which was entirely destroyed.

Muntazah Palace, the president's summer residence near Alexandria, stands out on the skyline

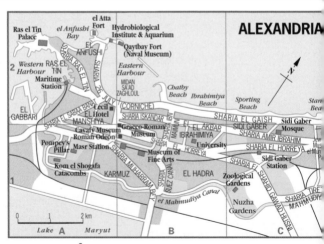

What to See in Alexandria

AMUD EL-SAWARI (POMPEY'S PILLAR) & SERAPEUM ✪✪

Pompey's Pillar is one of Alexandria's most famous landmarks. The Crusaders wrongly attributed this 27m-high pink granite column to Pompey. It was erected for Diocletian around AD 295, probably to support his equestrian statue. The hill on which it stands was ancient Rhakotis, where Alexander the Great first established Alexandria. The Serapeum and the great Alexandrian Library developed into a major centre of learning under the Ptolemies, and remained so until the 4th century when the Christians burned everything down. The pillar and two granite sphinxes are all that remain.

BIBILIOTHECA ALEXANDRINA ✪✪✪

Inspired by the ancient library founded in the 3rd century BC, the new library is designed to hold 8 million books, but the collection is far from complete yet. The circular design evokes the sun rising again on this side of the Mediterranean. The complex includes a good manuscript collection, a small antiquities museum, a concert hall and a planetarium.

KOM EL-DIKKA (ROMAN ODEON) ✪✪✪

Alexandria's multi-layered history can be seen at Kom el-Dikka (Arabic for pile of rubble). Beneath late Roman ruins, 9th- and 10th-century Muslim tombs and a late 18th-century fort, archaeologists revealed an elegant 2nd-century AD amphitheatre with marble seating for 750 people. Alexandrians enjoyed musical performances and wrestling contests at this pretty Roman theatre. The mosaic flooring in the forecourt originally covered the whole area.

🚩 52A1
✉ Sharia Amud el-Sawari
🕐 Daily 9–4
🚋 Tram 16 from Midan Zaghloul
💷 Cheap
🔁 Kom el-Shogafa Catacombs (➤ 54)

Above: *Roman theatre of Kom el-Dikka*

---

www.bibalex.org
🚩 52B1
✉ Corniche al-Bahr
🕐 Sun–Thu 11–6:30, Fri & Sat 3–6:30
🚋 Tram from Mahattat el-Raml
💷 Moderate; separate tickets for all museums

🚩 52A1
✉ Behind Cinema Amir, off Sharia Salman Yusuf
☎ 03-390 2904
🕐 Daily 9–4
💷 Cheap
🔁 Cavafy Museum (➤ 54), Graeco-Roman Museum (➤ 58), National Museum (➤ 58)

53

KOM EL-SHOGAFA CATACOMBS ✪✪✪

The catacombs at Kom el-Shogafa (Hill of Tiles) are unique both in plan and decoration, an unusual blend of ancient Egyptian, Greek and Roman designs which epitomised classical Alexandria's cosmopolitanism. The original 2nd century AD family vault was later enlarged to take in the community and thus created the largest Roman funerary complex found in Egypt.

The catacombs are on three levels, but the lowest floor is now inaccessible to visitors because of flooding. A wide staircase, lit by a central well through which corpses were lowered, leads through the first-floor vestibule to the Rotunda, where eight pillars support a domed roof, the Banquet Hall (to the left) and the Hall of Caracalla (to the right) with four painted tombs. A small spiral staircase leads to the eerie second-level tombs, which have wonderful decorations of bearded serpents, Medusas, a falcon Horus and the Egyptian gods Anubis and Sobek dressed as Roman soldiers.

MATHAF CAVAFY (CAVAFY MUSEUM) ✪

The apartment where the famous Greek poet Constantine Cavafy (1863–1933) lived for the last 25 years of his life has become a museum. 'Where could I live better?' he said. 'Below, the brothel caters for the flesh. And there is the church which forgives sin. And there is the hospital where we die.' His furniture, icons, death mask, books and the desk at which he wrote some of his greatest poetry, including *The City* and *The Barbarians,* can be seen.

➕ 52A1
☎ 03-484 5800
✉ Off Sharia Amud el-Sawari, Karmuz
🕐 Daily 9–4
👣 Moderate
↔ Pompey's Pillar (➤ 53)

Above: *the tomb decorations at Kom el-Shogafa are typically Alexandrian with a surprising blend of Egyptian and classical elements*

➕ 52A1
✉ 4 Sharia Sharm el-Sheikh, off Sharia Sultan Hussein
🕐 Tue–Sun 10–3 (Thu, Sun until 5). Closed Mon
👣 Free
↔ Kom el-Dikka (➤ 53), Graeco-Roman Museum (➤ 58)

Walk in Downtown Alexandria

Start at the Bibliotheca Alexandrina and walk west along the newly restored Corniche. Go past the Cecil Hotel, continue to the Tomb of the Unknown Soldier, then turn left.

This is the heart of the old European Alexandria, marked by an equestrian statue of Muhammad Ali.

At Midan el Tahrir turn left along Sharia Salah Salem.

Note the Moorish Anglican Church of St Mark and the National Bank of Egypt, a copy of Palazzo Farnese in Rome.

Continue along Sharia Fouad and at Patisserie Venous turn right into Sharia Nabi Danyal.

Half-way up the street, on the left, is Nabi Danyal Mosque built over a cistern, which is sometimes believed to contain Alexander the Great's tomb.

Turn left into Sharia Yussef with the Roman Odeon (➤ 53) on your left. After a visit continue along the same street and turn left round the site of the theatre. Cross the road into Sharia Zangalola.

This leads to the Greek Orthodox Church of St Saba.

Follow the street to the left of the church and then turn into the first street to the right, Sharia Sharm el–Sheikh. The Cavafy Museum is at No 4 (➤ 54). Walk left out of the museum, turn left onto Sharia Sultan Hussein, and then right into Sharia Nabi Danyal.

You will pass the Coptic Cathedral of St Mark (on the left) and Alexandria's neo-classical synagogue (on the right).

Continue along the street back to the Midan Zaghloul and have lunch at Trianon.

Distance
2½km

Time
2½ hours without visits, 4 hours with visits

Start Point
Bibliotheca Alexandrina, Corniche el-Bahr
➕ 52B1

End Point
Midan Sa'ad Zaghloul
➕ 52B2

Lunch
Trianon (££)
✉ 56 Midan Saad Zaghloul
☎ 03-483 5881

The balconied frontage of Alexandria's Cecil Hotel on the city's sweeping Corniche

Food & Drink

Egyptian cuisine is simple and basic, and is best enjoyed when prepared at home, or failing that, shared with friends in a reputable restaurant.

A table full of mezze including dips, salads, olives and pickles is more than a meal in itself

Wall paintings in ancient Egyptian tombs show large banquets with mounds of food and the pharaohs' descendants seemingly continue this tradition. Both at home and in restaurants huge amounts of food are served, to dazzle the appetite. Egyptians often share a number of *mezze* (appetisers) to accompany drinks or as a starter before a grill. Popular *mezze* include *wara'a aynab* (stuffed vine leaves), *tahina* (sesame paste), *baba ghanoug* (puréed aubergine with *tahina*), *hummus* (chickpea purée) and salads. *Aish baladi*, local flat bread, is often used to scoop up the food, instead of a fork.

National Dishes

Egyptian food has Syrian, Lebanese and Turkish influences. Stewed *fuul* or fava beans (➤ 99), drizzled with oil, spiced with chilli, cumin and lemon juice is eaten for breakfast or as a snack during the day. *Fuul* often comes with more beans, this time mashed, rolled into balls and fried, called *taamiya*. Vegetarians or carbohydrate fanatics love *kushari*, a mixture of macaroni, rice, fried onions, chickpeas and lentils, topped with a spicy tomato sauce and eaten any time of the day. More elaborate is *meloukhiya*, a spinach-like vegetable made into a thick soup with garlic, rabbit or chicken. Chicken and red meat are usually grilled, most often as kebab (lamb or beef skewers) or *kofta* (meatballs). Pigeon (*hamam*) is a delicacy, especially stuffed with wheat.

Egyptian patisseries sell an endless variety of sweets, candied fruits, chocolates and pastries

Sweets

The most popular oriental pastries are *basbousa* (oven-baked semolina cake soaked in honey), *baqlawa* (filo pastry stuffed with nuts and honey) and *kunafa* (angelhair stuffed either with thick cream, cream cheese or nuts). The best of Egyptian desserts is *Umm Ali*, a rich mixture of cracker bread, coconut, cream, nuts and raisins, soaked in hot milk. *Roz bi-laban* (rice pudding), *mahallabiya* (cornflour pudding) and *crème caramel* are standards on restaurant menus.

It is often more refreshing to drink a good cup of sweet mint tea than an icy cold drink

Café Pleasures

Tea is a good thirst quencher, even in the heat, and Arabian coffee with sugar (*qahwa mazbout*) soon becomes a habit, but cafés have other pleasures to offer. All year round there are fresh fruit juices (➤ 94), as well as a wide selection of soft drinks. Egyptians claim that 'once you drink from the Nile you will always come back', but it is wiser to stick to bottled mineral water. Traditional cafés also serve herbal infusions such as *yansoon* (anis), *helba* (fenugreek), *karkadeh* (hibiscus) and *'irfa* (cinnamon), and in winter try *sahlab*, a creamy concoction of arrowroot and cinnamon, usually topped with nuts and coconut.

Alcoholic Drinks

Although many Egyptians, as Muslims, do not drink alcohol, it is usually available wherever tourism is well established. Locally brewed Stella and Saqqara beers are very drinkable and some imported beers are available. The quality of Egyptian wine has improved over the last few years, and it comes in red, white, rosé and now even has a sparkling version. Most imported wines are sold at inflated prices, even in tax-free shops. Avoid local impersonations of famous-brand spirits – Johnny Talker, Marcel Horse and Ricardo.

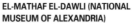

52B2

110 Tariq el-Hurreya

03-483 5519

Daily 9–5

Good

Moderate

Graeco-Roman Museum
(► 58), Kom el-Dikka
(► 53), Cavafy Museum
(► 54)

EL-MATHAF EL-DAWLI (NATIONAL MUSEUM OF ALEXANDRIA)

This interesting new museum, set in a beautiful white Italianate villa in Alexandria's city centre, is the first of a line of museums in important Egyptian cities. Its aim is to reveal the city's long and specific history, from antiquity until the modern period, through the very well displayed and labelled artefacts that have come from several of the city's other museums. The collection is laid out over three floors, the first of which is devoted to the Pharaonic

period. The second floor displays artefacts from the Graeco-Roman period and the top floor is devoted to Cotpic, Muslim and modern Alexandria. Highlights include the sphinx and other sculpture found in the Eastern harbour, wonderful Roman death masks, the small but elegant Tanagra terracotta statues and a bronze sculpture of Harpocrates in a mixed Greek and Egyptian style. Every room has several interesting panels explaining about ancient Egyptian rituals and gods, as well as the development of religion, art and history through the ages.

EL MATHAF EL-ROMANI (GRAECO-ROMAN MUSEUM)

This great museum has Egypt's largest collection of artefacts from the Graeco-Roman period (c331 BC–AD 300), mostly found

52B1

5 Sharia el-Mathaf

03-487 6434

Daily 9–4, Fri 9–11:30, 1:30–4

Café (£)

Moderate

Kom el-Dikka (► 53),
Cavafy Museum (► 54),
National Museum (► 58)

in and around Alexandria. At the time of writing there is a plan to close the museum down and rebuild it, but the date to reopen has not been set. The most important artefacts will be moved to other museums in the city. Highlights include the splendid 2nd-century AD black granite Apis bull and the statue of Serapis from the Serapeum. The museum has some exquisite Hellenistsic sculptures and a great collection of Tanagra, the small terracotta sculptures that were cast to celebrate youth and beauty.

MATHAF MAHMOUD SAID ✪✪

Mahmoud Said (1897-1964) was one of Egypt's finest 20th-century artists. About 40 of his unusual works, including his stunning Egyptian nudes, are beautifully exhibited in his own Italianate villa. Displayed on the first floor are the works of two of his contemporaries Saif and Adham Wanli, while a Museum of Modern Art fills the basement.

QASR EL-MUNTAZAH (MUNTAZAH PALACE) ✪✪

Khedive Abbas II's extravagant Turko-Florentine palace, now the presidential summer residence, is closed to the public, but the vast, beautiful gardens are a popular day trip for Alexandrian families. The private Muntazah beach is one of the most pleasant near Alexandria, separated from Ma'amoura bay by a pretty Turkish-style belvedere.

QAL'AT QAYTBAY (QAYTBAY FORT) ✪✪

The fabled lighthouse or Pharos of Alexandria, one of the Seven Wonders of the ancient world, was built in 279 BC by Sostratus for Ptolemy II. It was reputedly over 125m high and had over 300 rooms. The lighthouse was totally destroyed by earthquakes in the 11th and 14th centuries, but excavations have revealed several fragements of it. In 1479 Sultan Qaytbay built his fort on the site, reusing some of the Pharos's stones and columns, notably in the west-facing outer wall. The fort has great views from the walls.

🕆 Off map 52C2
✉ 6 Sharia Mohammed Said Pasha, Gianaclis
☎ 03–582 1688
🕐 Sat–Thu 9–1:30, 5–9
🎟 Cheap
🚃 Tram 2 to San Stefano stop

🕆 52C1
✉ Muntazah Bay
🍴 Fast food restaurants (£), restaurants at Helnan Palestine and Salamlek hotels (£££)
🚌 Bus 260 from Ramleh to Abu Qir
♿ Few   🎟 Cheap

🕆 52B2
✉ End of the Corniche
☎ 03-480 9144
🕐 Daily 9–4; closed Fri 11:30–1:30
🚌 Minibus No 706 or 707 from Midan Orabi or No 15 tram from Ramleh
🎟 Cheap
↪ Near by is Alexandria's lively fish market

Opposite: *Ptolemy I introduced the cult of Serapis – the god's shape came to him in a dream*

Left: *the Egyptian flag flies from the top of the 15th-century Qaytbay fort*

What to See in the Northwest

EL-ALAMEIN ⚙

Winston Churchill wrote: 'Before Alamein we never had a victory. After Alamein we never had a defeat.' The 1942 battle between the German Afrika Korps and the Allied Eighth Army at el-Alamein marked a turning point in World War II. Around 11,000 soldiers were killed, many of them are buried in the town's cemeteries. The War Museum illustrates with maps, uniforms and models the North Africa Campaign as well as the 1973 war between Egypt and Israel.

✚ 28B5
✉ 106km west of Alexandria
🕐 Museum daily 9–4, Commonwealth War Cemetery daily 7–4:30
🍴 Cafeteria at Al-Amana Hotel opposite museum (£–££) ☎ 046-493 8324
🚌 Buses from Alexandria to Mersa Matruh stop 200m from the War Museum, but no transport to the cemeteries
♿ Few
🎫 Museum cheap, cemeteries free

Anti-aircraft guns from World War II at the open-air section of el-Alamein's Military Museum

MERSA MATRUH ⚙

Mersa Matruh has grown from a sleepy fishing town into a sprawling, dull summer resort for Egyptian holidaymakers. In the summer the once superb beaches are now overcrowded and full of litter, and Western women may feel awkward bathing amongst fully clothed Egyptian women. Rommel's Beach, where the Desert Fox reputedly went for a swim, is slightly cleaner but the best beaches are some way west of town: Cleopatra's Beach (7km), El-Obeid Beach (20km) and the splendid Agibah Beach (28km) with deep turquoise water. The Rommel Museum, in a cave behind the port, has a collection of Rommel's memorabilia, including his maps and coat.

✚ 28B5
✉ 290km from Alexandria, 512km from Cairo
ℹ Corner of Sh. Omar Mukhtar/the Corniche ☎ 046 0493 1841
🍴 Beau Site Hotel/ Restaurant (££) on Sharia el-Shati ☎ 046-493 8555
🚌 Buses from Cairo and Alexandria
✈ Domestic flights from Cairo
♿ Few

RASHID (ROSETTA) ⚙

During the Ottoman era Rosetta had a larger port than Alexandria. Nowadays the town is neglected but the 22 surviving grand mansions bear witness to its glory days. Most of the houses, built in Delta-style architecture with red and black brickwork and elaborate wooden screens, have been restored or are under restoration. One of the finest, Ramadan House on Sharia Port Said, can be visited inside, while the neighbouring 18th-century houses can be

✚ 28C5
✉ 64km east of Alexandria
🕐 Houses and fort daily 9–4, Fri closed 12–1:30
🍴 Cafés (£) on main street
🚌 Hourly bus from Alexandria, Midan el-Gumhuriya
🎫 Cheap

admired from the outside. From there walk downhill and take the 2nd street to the left for some more stunning architecture: House of al-Toqati, House of Abu Shaheen and the superb House of Amasyali with wonderful painted ceilings. Five kilometres outside, Qaytbay's 15th-century fort marks the end of the Nile's 5,440km-long run from East Africa into the Mediterranean. Near here, in 1799, a French officer discovered a 2nd-century BC basalt stone with inscriptions in three scripts, hieroglyphs, demotic and Greek. It was from this Rosetta Stone (now in London's British Museum) that French scholar Jean François Champollion deciphered ancient Egyptian hieroglyphs.

A wonderful fresco of the Annunciation in the Church of el-Adhra (the Virgin) at Deir el-Suryani

WADI NATRUN ⭐⭐

Although monasticism started in the Eastern Desert (► 87), it was in Wadi Natrun that the rules were developed. For the last 1,500 years the Coptic popes have been chosen from these monasteries. The current pope, Shenuda III, formerly a monk at Deir el-Suryani, has encouraged a monastic revival. St Bishoi (AD 320–407) was one of the earliest monks in Wadi Natrun and his monastery still has more than 100 monks and several hermits. Deir el-Suryani was founded in the 6th-century by displeased monks from Deir Bishoi and later taken over by Syrian monks. Deir el-Suryani's Church of the Virgin has some magnificent frescoes and also the cave where St Bishoi prayed with his hair tied to the ceiling to keep him upright. The oldest and most remote of these monasteries is Deir Baramus, founded by two sons of Emperor Valentine who died during their fasting. Deir el-Maqar was founded by St Makarius, who died in AD 390 after spending 60 years as a hermit in the desert.

➕ 28C5
✉ 105km from Cairo, off Alexandria Desert Road
🕐 Check with Coptic Patriarchate ☎ 02-282 5374/284 3159 for opening times. Deir Anba Bishoi is open daily, Deir el-Maqar is closed to the public
🍴 Wadi Natrun Resthouse (£–££) on Desert Road
🚌 Buses between Cairo and Alexandria to the Resthouse, and from there regular pick-ups to the monasteries
✋ Donations appreciated
❓ Monasteries are closed during the five seasons of Fast (dates variable)

61

The Western Desert Oases

The Western Desert, covering some 3 million sq km, runs from the Mediterranean south to Kordofan in Central Sudan, and from the Nile Valley west to Fezzan in Libya.

What to See in the Oases

🔢 28B4
✉️ 360km from Cairo
🍴 Cafés/restaurant (£)
🚌 Daily buses Cairo from Tungoman bus station. Buses to Farafra on Sat, Mon, Thu between 1 and 2PM

Above: *farming in the fields of the oases is a labour-intensive job*

BAHARIYA   😊😊
On the main street of Bahariya's main town, el-Bawiti, is the Oasis Heritage Museum, with exhibits on Bedouin life and a little shop selling excellent local crafts. In the middle of the gardens (used to cultivate fruit trees) are the Roman el-Bishnu springs; however, these are not recommended for bathing. Instead, take a day trip to some of the desert springs or spend a night in the amazing White Desert en route to Farafra. Further along the oasis road is el-Qasr, built over Bahariya's ancient capital, with the remains of a Temple of Bes (664–525 BC) and a Roman Triumphal Arch.

🔢 28B2
✉️ 310km from Farafra
ℹ️ For information Midan al-Gamaa, Mut
☎️ 092-820 407
🍴 Cafés (£)
🚌 Daily buses from Cairo, Asyut, Kharga, Farafra, Bahariya
🎟️ Sights cheap
🕐 Museum: Sat–Thu 8–2

DAKHLA   😊😊😊
Mut, the ancient and modern capital, has a small Ethnographic Museum, with scenes of life in the oases, and hot springs believed to cure colds and rheumatism. Al-Qasr, about 30km from Mut, is Dakhla's medieval capital of three-storey mudbrick houses. The Ayyubid Nasr el-Din Mosque is notable for its 21m-high wooden minaret. Five kilometres further west are the beautifully decorated 1st and 2nd-century AD Muwazaka Tombs and 2km from there, the 1st-century AD Roman temple of Deir el-Haggar.

🔢 28B3
✉️ 180km from el-Bawiti, Bahariya
🍴 A few restaurants (£)
🚌 Daily buses from Cairo, Bahariya and Dakhla, except on Wed
❓ Tours to the White Desert from al-Waha Hotel

FARAFRA   😊😊
Qasr Farafra is the only settlement in this most beautiful oasis, with a small, pretty mudbrick museum built by local artist Badr. Walking in the peaceful palm groves and lovely gardens make up for a lack of ancient monuments.

DID YOU KNOW?

Despite growing tourism to the oases, the local people remain very traditional, and most women are still veiled. Visitors can show respect by dressing modestly, covering up arms and legs, avoid public display of affection between men and women, and women should not swim in the springs in the centre of the town.

KHARGA ⭐⭐

Modern Kharga town has borne the brunt of the government's New Valley development and has little charm, although the Kharga Museum of Antiquities is worth visiting to see well-labelled displays of locally found artefacts. North of the town, beyond the ruined Ptolemaic temple of Nadura, stands one of Egypt's few surviving Persian monuments, the 6th-century BC Temple of Hibis dedicated to Amun-Re. Near by is the impressive Bagawat necropolis with finely decorated Christian chapels from the 3rd to the 7th centuries AD. North of the necropolis, and only accessible by car, are two superb Roman fortresses and some remarkable aqueducts.

🚩 28C2
✉ 195km from Dakhla
ℹ Sharia Nasser
☎ 092-921 206
🕐 Museum daily 8–4; temples and necropolis daily 8–6 summer, 8–5 winter
🍴 Hotel restaurants (£–££)
🚌 Daily buses from Cairo, Asyut, and other oases
🚉 Fri train to Luxor
✈ Two flights a week from Cairo

SIWA ⭐⭐⭐

Siwa Town is still a sleepy, relaxed sort of place, despite the increase in visitors in recent years. The Traditional Siwan House shows what most Siwan houses looked like before breezeblock arrived. The new town lies in the shadow of abandoned Shali, the mudbrick hilltop town founded in 1203 and fortified against Bedouin attacks, which is floodlit at night. Alexander the Great came to Siwa in 331 BC to consult the Oracle at the ancient settlement of Aghurmi, 3km east of the modern town. The 26th Dynasty Temple of the Oracle dedicated to Amun-Re has survived well. From the minaret of Aghurmi's Mosque there are excellent views of this picturesque settlement, inhabited until the early 20th century, and over towards the nearby temple of Umm Ubayda. The salt lake Birket Siwa and Futnas Island are a favourite picnic spot and a good place to swim. The main attractions of Siwa however are the vast palm groves and the spectacular nearby Great Sand Sea with its high perfect sand dunes and cold and hot water springs.

www.siwa-safari.com
www.siwa-oasis.com
🚩 28A4
✉ 300km south of Mersa Matruh
ℹ Siwa town
☎ 046-460 2338
🍴 Cafés/restaurants (£–££)
🚌 2 daily buses from Mersa Matruh and Alexandria
❓ Siwa Festival 3 days in October just before the date harvest; Traditional Siwan House is open Sat–Wed 10–noon

Above: *a blue version of a pilgrim's trip by boat to Mecca from Siwa*

Nile Valley &
Lake Nasser

In a land with little rain, ancient Egyptians recognised that the Nile's annual summer flooding was a blessing, and so organised themselves to make the most of the flood and the fertile silt it left as it receded. In the process they created the model for society as we know it; a hierarchy of workers, administrators and higher management (pharaohs) that also made possible the construction of huge temples and tombs. The annual flooding created seasons of field work and enforced rest, which characterised life in the Egyptian countryside until the end of the 19th century. The completion of the two Aswan dams (1902 and 1965), which lost Nubia beneath Lake Nasser, ended that annual cycle of drought and flood. In spite of the many changes that have followed, the Nile remains as much Egypt's lifeline as it was in the past.

> '*...anyone who sees Egypt,
> without having heard a word
> about it before, must
> perceive... that the Egypt to
> which the Greeks go in their
> ships is an acquired country,
> the gift of the river...*'

HERODOTUS
The Histories
*c*460 BC

———————•———————

Ramses II at Luxor Temple, staring into eternity

Luxor

Luxor is built over part of ancient Thebes, also known as Waset or Apet. One of the great cities of the ancient world, Thebes spread across both sides of the Nile and was the political capital of Egypt during the Middle and New Kingdoms. Some of the most famous pharaohs – Ramses II, Seti I, Hatshepsut, Tutankhamun – lived here and left their mark. Long after political power passed to the north, Theban temples remained the centre of religious influence thanks to huge gifts of land, gold and revenues, particularly to Amun's main temple at Karnak. The glory of Thebes was still very real when the Greek poet Homer wrote about its 100 gates, but the 6th-century BC Persian King Cambyses hastened its long decline by setting fire to everything that could be burned. Most of what has survived that and the ravages of centuries are the remains of stone temples and rock-cut tombs.

The Temple of Luxor, right in the heart of the modern town, is difficult to miss

Early Christians defaced many temple images and converted some of the courts into churches, while Arab Muslims, whose religion banned the representation of people, generally showed no interest in the ruins. Difficulties of Nile travel for foreigners gave Thebes and the rest of the Upper Nile valley a legendary status in the West. Its rediscovery, starting in earnest in the 18th century and continuing today (KV5, the largest tomb so far found in Egypt, is the latest to be excavated in the Valley of the Kings) has attracted many visitors from around the world. As a result, Luxor has grown from a village in the 1860s to become a small town in 1895, and today it is a busy modern city.

What to See on the East Bank

KARNAK (► 20–1, TOP TEN)

MA'BAD EL-UQSUR (LUXOR TEMPLE)   ✪✪✪

The Temple of Luxor or the 'harem of the south', like nearby Karnak, is dedicated to the Theban triad of Amun-Min, Mut and Khonsu, but it is a far more coherent building as fewer pharaohs have made additions. During the Opet (fertility) festival, a procession of holy barges brought Amun's statue from Karnak to Luxor, where he was united with his wife Mut to ensure an excellent harvest. The mosque built over part of the temple is dedicated to Luxor's patron saint Abu el-Haggag, during whose moulid (► 116) feluccas are pulled around the temple, perhaps a reminder of the ancient festival.

The First Pylon, built by Ramses II, features his favourite theme of victory at the battle of Kadesh. His two colossi, a ruined standing statue and one of two splendid obelisks (the other one now adorns the Place de la Concorde in Paris) flank the entrance. In the Court of Ramses II there is an interesting relief of the temple itself and, to the right, a funerary procession led by Ramses II's many sons. Beyond the Second Pylon the impressive Colonnade of Amenhotep III leads to the wide Court of Amenhotep III and a small Hypostyle Hall. The inner sanctum contains a number of shrines, including a columned portico used as a chapel by Roman soldiers, Alexander the Great's Sanctuary of the Sacred Barge and to the left Amenhotep III's Birth Room, near which the cache of statues now on view in the Luxor Museum (► 68) were found.

➕ 29D2
✉ Corniche
🕐 Daily 6AM–10PM in summer, 6AM–9PM in winter (best explored in daylight, but try to return at night when spotlights add to the atmosphere and accentuate the carvings)
👤 Moderate
↔ Karnak (► 20–21), Mummification Museum (► 68)
❓ Son et lumière shows every evening at 6, 7:15, 8:30, and 9:45 on weekends

Above: vertical grooves along the pylon façade of Luxor Temple supported flagpoles, while the openings above them were for the braces holding the poles

🕂 29D2
✉ Corniche
☎ 095-381 501
⏰ Daily 9–1, 5–10 (5–9 in winter)
♿ Few
🏛 Moderate
↔ Luxor Temple (► 67), Luxor Museum (► 68)

🕂 29D2
✉ Corniche
☎ 095-380 269
⏰ Daily 9–1, 6–10 in summer, 9–1, 6–9 in winter
♿ Few
🏛 Moderate; additional ticket (cheap) for New Hall
↔ Luxor Temple (► 67), Mummification Museum (► 68)

Egyptian art students sketching some of the well-displayed collection of antiquities at the Luxor Museum

MATHAF EL-MUMIA (MUMMIFICATION MUSEUM) ✪✪

Luxor's mummification museum (also ► 110), the first of its kind in the world, houses a unique collection of mummies, including mummified animals such as cats, fish and crocodiles, as well as tools used for mummification. Everything is well displayed and labelled, giving a clear insight into the whole mummification process.

MATHAF EL-UQSUR LI-L-ATHAAR (LUXOR MUSEUM) ✪✪✪

This small modern museum is one of the finest in Egypt and most exhibits are from local temples and tombs. What sets it apart is that displays are carefully chosen, well-labelled and perfectly lit, to make the most of their beauty. Much of the ground floor is dedicated to New Kingdom statues, including a superb bust of the young Tuthmosis III (No 61) and a bizarre alabaster statue of the crocodile god Sobek holding Amenhotep III (No 107).

The upper floor has a beautiful mural from Akhenaten's temple at Karnak, with the king and his wife worshipping the sun god Aten. A glass case shows some objects from Tutankhamun's tomb in the Valley of the Kings (► 18), including two fine model boats, a superb gold-inlaid cow's head, sandals and arrows. The New Hall displays the cache of 26 statues found in 1989, near Amenhotep III's Birth Room in Luxor Temple.

What to See on the West Bank

BIBAN EL-HARIM (VALLEY OF THE QUEENS) ⦿⦿

Known in ancient times as the 'place of beauty', this was the resting place of more than 80 queens and princes from the 18th to the 20th Dynasties (1570–1070 BC), many of whom have not been identified. The tombs are far less grand and elaborate than those in the Valley of the Kings, and many were left unfinished, suggesting that queens and their offspring were considerably less important than the pharaohs themselves. The tomb of Nefertari, the wife of Ramses II, is the exception, and its exquisite paintings have been restored. Several sons of Ramses III died young of smallpox and, unusually, the reliefs in their tombs show them being led by their father through the underworld.

+ 69A2
⊠ 3km south of the Valley of the Nobles
🕐 Daily 6AM–7PM in summer, 7–5 in winter
✋ Tickets for Nefertari's tomb when open are limited to 150 a day, and are expensive; the other three tombs open to the public are moderate
↔ Deir el-Medina (► 70), Medinat Habu (► 72)
❓ Some tombs may be closed for restoration

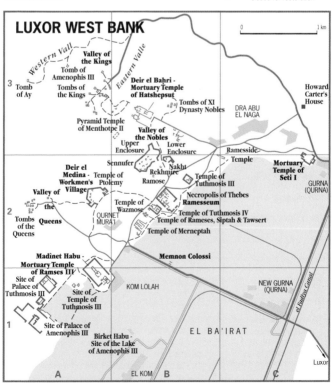

LUXOR WEST BANK

0   1 km

Western Valley

Valley of the Kings

Tomb of Amenophis III

3   Tomb of Ay

Tombs of the Kings

Eastern Valley

Deir el Bahri - Mortuary Temple of Hatshepsut

Tombs of XI Dynasty Nobles

Howard Carter's House

DRA ABU EL NAGA

Pyramid Temple of Menthotpe II

Valley of the Nobles

Upper Enclosure

Lower Enclosure

Ramesside Temple

Deir el Medina - Workmen's Village

Sennufer

Temple of Ptolemy

Nakht
Rekhmire
Ramose

Temple of Tuthmosis III

Mortuary Temple of Seti I

GURNA (QURNA)

Valley of the Queens

Temple of Wazmose

Ramesseum

Necropolis of Thebes

Temple of Tuthmosis IV

QURNET MURA'I

Tombs of the Queens

Temple of Rameses, Siptah & Tawsert

Temple of Merneptah

Madinet Habu - Mortuary Temple of Ramses III

Memnon Colossi

Site of Palace of Tuthmosis III

Site of Temple of Tuthmosis III

KOM LOLAH

NEW GURNA (QURNA)

el Fadrat Canal

Site of Palace of Amenophis III

Birket Habu - Site of the Lake of Amenophis III

EL BA'IRAT

Luxor

A   EL KOM   **B**   EL KOM   **C**

🚩 69B3
⊠ West Bank
🕐 Daily 6AM–7PM in
summer, 7–5 in winter
✋ Moderate; tickets must
be bought from the
central Antiquities
Inspectorate Office, 3km
inland (🚩 69B2), and are
sold per group of tombs
↔ Ramesseum (➤ 73), Deir
el-Bahri (➤ below)

*Opposite: relief showing
the falcon-headed sun
god in the mortuary
temple of Hatshepsut*

🚩 69B3
⊠ West Bank
🕐 Daily 6AM–7PM in
summer, 7–5 in winter
✋ Moderate (➤ above
Biban el-Nubalaa)
↔ Ramesseum (➤ 73),
Valley of the Nobles
(➤ above)
❓ It is possible to walk over
the hill, or take a donkey,
to the Valley of the Kings
(➤ 18) with fantastic
views over Luxor and the
monuments

🚩 69A2
⊠ West Bank
🕐 Daily 6AM–7PM in
summer, 7–5 in winter
✋ Moderate (➤ above
Biban el-Nubalaa)
↔ Ramesseum (➤ 73),
Madinat Habu (➤ 72),
Valley of the Queens (➤ 69)

BIBAN EL-MULUK (VALLEY OF THE KINGS)
(➤ 18, TOP TEN)

BIBAN EL-NUBALAA
(TOMBS OF THE NOBLES)

Whilst the pharaohs' tombs were decorated with religious texts, those of the nobles depict the good life they had led on earth in the hope that it would continue after their death. The result is often more satisfying than the royal tombs. It is easy to imagine these peoples' lives and interests, because their tombs show scenes of family life, agriculture, and how they imagined the afterlife, including the boat journey to Abydos and funerary banquets. As the quality of limestone was too poor for carvings, these scenes were painted on plaster. Three groups of tombs are particularly worth visiting for their amazing and well-preserved paintings: Nakht and Menna; Rekhmire and Sennofer; Ramose, Userhat and Khaemhat.

DEIR EL-BAHARI (MORTUARY TEMPLE OF HATSHEPSUT)

Dramatically set against the Theban hills, this splendid temple built by Queen Hatshepsut's architect (and perhaps also her lover) Senenmut, always surprises with its simplicity and almost modern look. Queen Hatshepsut was one of the few female pharaohs to reign over Egypt, taking power from her stepson, Tuthmosis III, when her husband Tuthmosis II died. The temple terraces were filled with exotic trees and fountains, and linked to the Nile by an avenue of Sphinxes. The colonnades of the Lower Terrace were defaced by Tuthmosis III, but the Middle Terrace colonnades are fascinating with the Birth Colonnade, confirming the Queen's divine parentage, and the Punt Colonnade, depicting her journey to Punt (probably in today's Somalia). Beyond lies the Chapel of Hathor with bovine Hathor columns. The recently restored Higher Terrace has the Sanctuary of Amun hewn into the rock.

DEIR EL-MEDINA (WORKERS' VILLAGE)

Artists and artisans worked on tombs in the Valley of the Kings (➤ 18) for ten days at a time before returning to their family home in Deir el-Medina, where they built their own tombs. The tomb of Sennedjem has very fine wall-paintings of agricultural scenes, Sennedjem and his wife in front of the gods, and a depiction of the tree of life from which a goddess appears. The tomb of Ankherha is equally brightly painted with scenes of Ankherha's family with lots of children.

✚ 69B2
✉ Gurna
🕐 6AM–7PM in summer, 7–5 in winter
🖐 Moderate (➤ 72 Biban el-Nubalaa
↔ Ramesseum (➤ 73), Valley of the Nobles (➤ 70)

✚ 69C2
✉ Gurna
🕐 6AM–7PM in summer, 7–5 in winter
🖐 Moderate (➤ 72 Biban el-Nubalaa
↔ Deir el-Bahari (➤ 70)

Below: *the well-preserved temple of Madinat Habu*

✚ 69A2
✉ Kom Lolah
🕐 6AM–7PM in summer, 7–5 in winter
🍴 Outside the gates two cafés serve lunch (£)
🖐 Moderate (➤ 72 Biban el-Nubalaa)
↔ Deir el-Medina (➤ 70), Memnon Colossi (➤ 73)

MA'BAD MERNEPTAH (TEMPLE OF MERNEPTAH)

Merneptah, son of Ramses II, ruled for only 10 years from 1213 BC, and very little remains of his funerary temple. However the Swiss mission who worked on the temple for over 30 years has opened a small but interesting museum that clearly explains the history and lay out of the site. There are displays of statues, sphinxes and reliefs, some with the original colour, uncovered during excavations.

MA'BAD SETI (TEMPLE OF SETI I) ✪✪

Dedicated to the god Amun and to Seti's father Ramses I, this largely destroyed temple still shows the hallmark of Seti I (1291–1278 BC) with some of the finest wall decorations and reliefs of the New Kingdom. The first two pylons and courts have disappeared and today only the temple proper remains. A colonnade leads into a Hypostyle Hall with columns decorated with reliefs of Seti I and Ramses I making offerings to the gods. The chapel to the left of the temple's main entrance is dedicated to Ramses I, who died before a temple could be built for him.

MADINAT HABU
(MORTUARY TEMPLE OF RAMSES III) ✪✪✪

Ramses III (1182–1151 BC) modelled this impressive temple on his forefather Ramses II's mortuary temple (Ramesseum, ➤ opposite). Madinat Habu is not on many tourists' itinerary, even though it was the last classical pharaonic temple built, with very few later additions. The vast temple complex is entered through a high gatehouse, built as a Syrian-style fortress, and the steps lead to the pharaoh's pleasure apartments with a good view over the

grounds. The magnificent First Pylon records battles that Ramses III never fought, most likely copied from Ramses II's temple. The First and Second Courts are vast and lined with images of Ramses III making offerings to the gods, but the Hypostyle Hall and Inner Sanctuaries were severely damaged during an earthquake in 27 BC. Take a walk along the outer walls, decorated with more giant reliefs of Ramses III fishing, hunting or at war.

Below: *the head of the statue of Ramses II ruined part of the Ramesseum when it fell*

MEMNON COLOSSI ⭐⭐

Amenhotep III's (1386–1349 BC) giant colossi overlook green fields – their faces as well as the mortuary temple they guarded, disappeared long ago. A crack in one of the statues led the Greeks to believe this was Memnon singing to Eos, hence the name; it was repaired in AD 199. Smaller statues of Queen Tiy and Amenhotep III's mother, Mutemuia, flank the pharaoh's legs and the sides of the seats are decorated with sunken reliefs of round-bellied Nile gods with papyrus and lotus flowers.

✚ 69B2
✉ The main road to the ticket office
🕓 6AM–7PM in summer, 7–5 in winter
🖐 Moderate (➤ 72 Biban el-Nubalaa

RAMESSEUM ⭐⭐

Ramses II (1279–1212 BC) built magnificent temples, including large parts of Karnak (➤ 20–21) and Luxor Temple (➤ 67) and two temples at Abu Simbel, but his own mortuary temple fell because it was built on weak foundations. The temple entrance leads to the First Pylon decorated with scenes from the Battle at Kadesh. Near the Second Pylon, is the base of the statue of 'Ozymandias' (a Greek mis-reading of one of Ramses's titles), which inspired the British poet Shelley. Once the largest statue in the world, weighing over 900 tonnes, it ruined the Second Court when it fell. The head and part of the torso remain where they landed; other parts are now in museums all over the world. The Hypostyle Hall is decorated with battle scenes, and the ceiling of the Astronomic Room is painted with the oldest known 12-month calendar.

✚ 69B2
✉ Opposite the Tombs of the Nobles
🕓 6AM–7PM in summer, 7–5 in winter   🖐 Moderate

What to See in Central Nile Valley

This area may be subject to security alerts (► 122, Personal Safety).

ABYDOS (► 16, TOP TEN)

BENI HASAN ✪✪

Beni Hasan is a Middle Kingdom necropolis on the east bank of the river, with four tombs open to the public. They belonged to local governors and are remarkable for their elegant columns and fine paintings on stucco. These depict scenes from daily life, agriculture and hunting, as well as more unusual acrobats and wrestlers.

DANDARA, TEMPLE OF HATHOR ✪✪✪

The beautiful Temple of Hathor was built between 125 BC and AD 60 as part of an attempt by the Ptolemies and the Romans to reinforce their position by claiming association with the ancient Egyptian gods. There was probably an earlier temple of Hathor here, as this was the site where Hathor was believed to have given birth to Horus's son. During the New Year festival, Hathor's statue was taken in procession to the roof, where it was exposed to the sun god Re before being escorted to the temple at Edfu (► 80) to be reunited with Horus. Scenes of this festival decorate the temple walls, as well as reliefs of Roman emperors performing ancient Egyptian rituals. The carvings are much cruder than earlier pharaonic work, but the temple has been well-preserved and remains impressive.

✚ 28C3
✉ 20km south of el-Minya
◔ Daily 8–5
🚍 Private taxi from Minya, most probably with a police escort, then ferry across
✋ Cheap

✚ 29D3
✉ 4km across the Nile from Qena, 64km north of Luxor
◔ Daily 7–6
🍴 Café (£)
🚍 Train to Qena, then taxi; service taxi or cruise boat from Luxor
✋ Moderate

Palm trees grow in what was the Sacred Lake of the Temple of Hathor

Fascinating scenes of daily life in the rock tombs of Beni Hasan

EL-MINYA ✪

The provincial town of Minya was a good base for visiting the surrounding antiquities until the 1990s when it became a hothouse for Islamic militants. Things have calmed down and it is again a pleasant place to be, but the police presence has remained. The town has a few dilapidated colonial buildings and an interesting Muslim and Coptic cemetery, Zawiyet el-Mayyetin, on the West Bank to which the dead were transported on feluccas until not long ago.

✚ 28C4
✉ 245km south of Cairo
ℹ Governorate Building, Corniche el-Nil, Luxor
☎ 086-371 521
🚆 Trains from Cairo

SOHAG ✪

Sohag is a small town with a large Coptic community. Its main attractions are the nearby monasteries on the edge of the desert. Deir el-Abyad (White Monastery), founded in the 5th century by St Pjol and dedicated to St Shenuda, looks like a pharaonic temple. Once it was a thriving community of more than 2,000 monks, but only a few remain today. The smaller Deir el-Ahmar (Red Monastery) was founded by St Bishoi, a disciple of St Shenuda.

✚ 29D3
✉ 206km south of el-Minya, 472km south of Cairo
🕐 Monasteries open daily 8–8 (free but donations welcome)
🚆 Trains from Cairo, Asyut, el-Minya and Luxor; monasteries reached by taxi only

TELL EL-AMARNA ✪✪

The fascinating city founded by the rebellious pharaoh Akhenaten (1350–1334 BC) and his beautiful wife Nefertiti, was abandoned after 14 years, when the king died, and the priests from Karnak destroyed it. They had left Thebes to establish Akhetaten, their new capital, dedicated to the sun god Aten. The Royal Road passes the ruins of the Great Temple of Aten, the Royal Residence, the State Palace and the Sanctuary of Aten. On the other side of the landing post are the better preserved Temple of Nefertiti and the Northern Tombs of Amarna nobles with scenes representing the joyful life at the capital. The Southern Tombs (14km) are the finest, especially those of Mahu and Ay.

✚ 28C3
✉ 60km south of el-Minya
🕐 Daily 8–4 in winter, 8–5 in summer
🚆 Taxi from Minya or Asyut, probably with police escort, then tourist ferry or normal ferry across
🎫 Tickets at the tourist office near the landing; prices vary. Bus tours are available as the site is large

TUNA EL-GEBEL ✪✪

Only a small area of the vast necropolis is open to the public. Near the entrance is the Sacred Animal Necropolis for mummified baboons, ibises and other animals. Further south is the City of Dead, where the tomb of High Priest Petosiris (300 BC) has fine wall-paintings of agriculture, crafts and funerary processions.

✚ 28C3
✉ 50km south of el-Minya
🕐 Daily 8–5
🚆 Taxi only, with police escort
🎫 Moderate

75

Camels with their attendants resting as they await tourists on the outskirts of the southern city of Aswan

Aswan

Aswan, Egypt's southernmost town, feels more like Africa than the rest of Egypt. The people, mostly Nubians, are taller and darker than Upper Egyptians, their music and culture has more in common with the Sudan than with Cairo or Alexandria, and the air smells sweet and tropical. Two deserts, the Eastern Desert and the Sahara, close in on the Nile which here flows around a series of granite rocks and little islands. The First Cataract, which ancient Egyptians believed was the source of the Nile, once marked the end of the civilised world, as boats were unable to pass this natural barrier. Yebu on Elephantine Island was the Old Kingdom frontier, as well as an important cult centre. Today, as in ancient times, Aswan is renowned for its wonderful winter climate and beautiful setting.

What to See in Aswan

29D2
West Bank of Nile
Closed to the public
Felucca, no public ferries

AGA KHAN MAUSOLEUM   ✪✪

This small but dignified mausoleum was built for Mohammed Shah Aga Khan (1877–1957), the leader of the Ismailis, a Shi'ite Muslim sect. The Aga Khan, who was famous for his incredible wealth, fell in love with this spot and with Aswan. His widow used to spend winters in the villa below the mausoleum but since her death in 2000 she lies buried beside him. The views over the Nile and Aswan are spectacular, especially at sunset.

The Nilometer was essential in fixing the level of taxes, which depended on the height of the Nile flood

MATHAF EL-ATHAAR (ASWAN ANTIQUITIES MUSEUM) ✪✪

Housed in the villa of Sir William Willcocks, the British engineer who designed the old Aswan dam, the museum has a massive collection of objects found on Elephantine Island and a collection of artefacts salvaged from the flooded areas beyond the dam. Pottery, jewellery and statues from the Middle and New Kingdom are displayed on the ground floor, while there are some mummies in the basement and a superb gold-covered statue of Khnum. By the Nile is the Nilometer with Greek, Roman, pharaonic and Arabic numerals, the most important instrument as taxes were calculated according to the height of the Nile. Further south are the ruins of ancient Yebu. Beyond a gateway on which Alexander II is shown worshipping Khnum are the ruins of a 30th Dynasty Temple of Khnum. Although this site is still being excavated, it is worth a visit for the spectacular views of Aswan and the Nile.

➕ 29D2
✉ On tip of Elephantine Island
🕐 Daily 7–4 winter, 7–5 summer
🚢 Ferry from the landing dock near EgyptAir office
♿ Moderate, includes visit to the Nilometer and ruins of Yebu

MATHAF EL-NUBA (NUBIA MUSEUM) ✪✪✪

The Nubia Museum is a long-awaited tribute to the Nubian people whose lands were flooded after the construction of the Aswan Dam. In a beautiful modern building vaguely inspired by traditional Nubian architecture, the museum's well-displayed, well-labelled exhibits follow the history, art and culture of Nubia from prehistoric times (c4500 BC) to the present day. Among the highlights are the oldest skeleton found in the Toshka region, a superb statue of a 25th Dynasty Kushite priest of Amun and an interesting display explaining the development of irrigation along the Nile. There is a reconstructed Nubian house in the museum garden.

➕ 29D2
✉ Sharia Abtal el-Tahrir
☎ 097-313 826
🕐 Daily 9–1, 5–9
♿ Few
▣ Moderate
❓ No photography

Felucca sailing around the Islands

Feluccas
Official prices for feluccas per person for every possible excursion including waiting time, are available from the tourist office:

 Midan el-Mahatta
☎ 097-312 811

Distance
3km

Time
3–4 hours with stops

Start point
Docks by EgyptAir office on the Corniche

End Point
Old Cataract Hotel

Feluccas sailing in the late afternoon sun, seen from the Old Cataract Hotel's terrace

Rent a felucca from the docks near the EgyptAir office. Late afternoon is best, when the air is cooler and the light is softer, in time to catch the sunset in all its majesty. Early morning is recommended if you want to visit the tombs on the way.

On the west bank are the Tombs of the Nobles (◐ 7–4, till 5 in summer), which belonged to the princes and priests of Elephantine. The finest are the tombs of Sirenput I and II, with colourful scenes of daily life. Higher up is the tomb of a local *sheikh* (saint) known as the Qubbat el-Hawa (Dome of the Winds), with fantastic views of Aswan. Continue by felucca to the Botanical Gardens on Kitchener's Island (open 8–sunset), a lush, sweet-smelling island presented to the British general Lord Kitchener after his military successes in Sudan. Kitchener decided to have the island planted with exotic plants and trees from all over the world.

Sailing around the back of the Elephantine Island, you should catch a glimpse of village life, including little children who sing Nubian songs from their tiny boats hoping for some *baksheesh* (tips). On the west bank beyond Elephantine, the Aga Khan's Mausoleum (► 76) is also the stop for the 10th-century St Simeon's Monastery (◐ 7–4, till 5 in summer), destroyed in 1173 by Saladin. The steep climb (½ hour) through soft sand is rewarded by the spectacular, romantic setting of this roofless basilica. End by jumping off at the Old Cataract Hotel landing (► 103) for an apéritif on the terrace.

EL-MESALLA EL-NAQSA (UNFINISHED OBELISK) ✪

This might have been the largest obelisk ever, 41m high and weighing almost 1,200 tonnes, but it was left unfinished in the quarry when a flaw in the granite was discovered. It was meant to be one of a pair, the other of which is the Lateran Obelisk, erected in the Temple of Tuthmosis III in Karnak but now in Rome.

29D2
🖂 2km south of Aswan on the road to Philae
🕔 Daily 7–4 (5 in summer)
Moderate

PHILAE TEMPLES (► 25, TOP TEN)

EL-SADD EL-ALI (HIGH DAM) ✪✪

The old Aswan dam, completed by the British in 1902, was soon found to be too small, but it wasn't until the 1960s that a new dam was built. President Nasser saw the High Dam as the key to making Egypt self-reliant, as controlling the Nile flood would provide electricity for the whole country. The High Dam is immense; 111m high, more than 3.8km long, 980m wide at the base, 40m at the top with a volume some 17 times that of the Pyramid of Khufu. Lake Nasser, the world's largest reservoir, at over 6,000sq km, has saved Egypt from famine and floods several times, and made it possible to irrigate vast stretches of desert. But it isn't all good news. As a result of the dam Nubians lost their land, ancient monuments were inundated by the lake (some were rescued by a UNESCO salvage operation), Nile silt no longer fertilises Egyptian fields and the ground-water level has risen, threatening monuments all along the Nile in Egypt.

29D2
🖂 7km south of the old Aswan dam
Few
Cheap
↔ Philae Temples (► 25)
❓ Photography of the dam is strictly forbidden, passport may be required

The enormous concrete structure of the High Dam, with the Russian-Egyptian Friendship Monument in the background

What to See in the Southern Nile Valley

DARAW ✪✪

The only reason people stop at Daraw is to visit its large camel market. Camels are brought across the desert along the Forty Days Road from Darfur and Kordofan in Sudan, to a place north of Abu Simbel. From there they are driven to Daraw and sometimes to Birqash near Cairo (➤ 45). The market is a fascinating place, especially in the early morning, when Sudanese traders in their traditional costumes prefer to do their business.

EDFU (TEMPLE OF HORUS) ✪✪✪

After Karnak (➤ 20–1), this is the largest temple in Egypt and also the best-preserved, having been buried in the sand and houses built over it until archaeologists uncovered it in the 1860s. Begun in 237 BC by Ptolemy III and dedicated to the falcon god Horus, the temple stands on the site where Horus is believed to have fought his uncle Seth for control of the world. Much has been learned about this temple from building and foundation texts inscribed on the walls.

The entrance is now at the back of the complex, but the visit should start at the Grand Pylon to the south. On the outside Neos Dionysos (Ptolemy XIII) is shown slaughtering his enemies in front of Horus. The inner walls portray the annual Festival of the Beautiful Meeting, when Horus's statue was taken to Hathor's temple at Dandara (➤ 74). Two impressive statues of Horus front the Hypostyle Hall, which leads into the beautifully decorated Festival Hall and Hall of Offerings, the oldest part of the temple. The Sanctuary still contains the granite altar on which rested Horus's sacred boat, and the large granite shrine which the statue of the god once inhabited.

✚	29D2
✉	40km north of Aswan, 5km south of Kom Ombo
◷	Every day before noon, but Sun morning is best, with the most camels
⛟	Minibus or service taxi from Aswan to Kom Ombo

✚	29D2
✉	115km south of Luxor, 105km north of Aswan
◷	Daily 7–5 summer, 7–4 in winter
🍴	Café (£)
⛟	Private taxi or tour, with police escort
♿	Moderate

Granite carving of the falcon god Horus at Edfu Temple

ESNA TEMPLE 😊😊

The temple of the ram-headed god Khnum was probably as large as Edfu after the reconstruction by Ptolemy VI (c180 BC), but most of it remains hidden under the village. Only the Hypostyle Hall, a 1st-century AD addition by the Roman emperor Claudius, has been excavated. Its 24 painted columns with capitals in the shape of different flowers and plants form an enclosed garden, while Roman emperors adorn the walls, making offerings to the Egyptian deities.

➕ 29D2
✉ 54km south of Luxor, 155km north of Aswan
🕐 Daily 7–4 (till 5 in summer)
🚌 Private taxi or tour, with police escort
💷 Cheap

KOM OMBO TEMPLE 😊😊

Most Egyptian temples were dedicated to a single deity, but Kom Ombo Temple, started by Ptolemy VI (c180 BC) and finished by Roman emperor Augustus (30 BC–AD 14), was dedicated to two: Horus the Elder and Sobek. The eastern side was devoted to the crocodile god Sobek, and the Chapel of Hathor near the entrance housed some mummified crocodiles. The other side of the temple was dedicated to Horus the Elder, known as the 'Good Doctor', and attracted sick pilgrims, who took part in complicated rituals here in the hope of a cure. The temple's dramatic location, on a bend in the river, was also its undoing – much of the pylon and the forecourt were swept away by the Nile, though a double entrance to the inner Hypostyle Hall survives with elegant floral columns. Behind the two sanctuaries there are seven chapels on whose outer walls is depicted an interesting display of medical instruments, clear evidence that ancient Egyptian surgeons performed highly sophisticated operations.

➕ 29D2
✉ 170km south of Luxor, 45km north of Aswan
🕐 Daily 7–5 (7–4 in winter)
🍴 Kiosk with drinks (£)
🚌 Private taxi or tour, with police escort
💷 Moderate
↔ Daraw (► 80)

Detail of fine reliefs on the columns of the twin temples dedicated to Horus and Sobek at Kom Ombo

Below: *visitors are dwarfed by the colossal Osirid statues of Ramses II in his temple at Abu Simbel*

Lake Nasser

UNESCO relocated many Nubian temples threatened by the building of the High Dam and the creation of Lake Nasser. For many years, fishing boats and the occasional ferry to Sudan had the lake to themselves, but several cruise ships (➤ 103) now operate between Aswan and Abu Simbel, fishing trips are increasingly popular (➤ 114) and several luxury hotels are planned.

What to See at Lake Nasser

ABU SIMBEL

The two temples at Abu Simbel were built by Ramses II and are the most spectacular Nubian monuments. The façade of the Great Temple of Re-Harakhte is dominated by four magnificent seated colossi of Ramses II, cut into the cliff, flanked by other members of the royal family. The Hypostyle Hall, lined with 10m-high Osirid statues of the pharaoh, is decorated with superb reliefs of his famous victories. The temples were hand-sawn out of the rock-face, cut into 1,050 blocks and reconstructed on an artificial hill, the inside of which can be visited (entrance beside the temple). Near by is the smaller Temple of Hathor fronted by statues of Ramses II and Nefertari with their children. The Hypostyle Hall, supported by Hathor-headed columns, has reliefs of the queen watching her husband at war. A cow statue of Hathor in the sanctuary is decorated with reliefs of Nefertari and Ramses.

29D1

280km south of Aswan

6AM–6PM summer (till 5 summer) or until the last plane leaves

Café (£)

Buses from Aswan

From Cairo and Aswan; return tickets include transfers between airport and site. If outgoing plane is delayed there may be little time at site

Expensive

22 Feb and 22 Oct at dawn the sun rays touch the cult statues; sound and light show (097-312 811)

The elegant Roman Kiosk of Qertassi with four papyrus and two Hathor-headed columns

AMADA ⭐

The oldest Egyptian temple in Nubia, Amada was built by Tuthmosis III and Amenhotep II, dedicated to Amun-Re and Re-Harakhte. Reliefs in the inner right-hand chapel show the temple's foundation rituals. In the sand lie early drawings of animals (including elephants) carved on stone. Near by is the Rock Temple of el-Derr, built by Ramses II, with excellent colourful reliefs, and the rock-cut Tomb of Penne, viceroy of Nubia under Ramses VI, with traditional themes on the walls.

➕ 29D1
✉ 170km south of the High Dam
🕐 Daily 6–6
🚢 Cruise boat only
 Free

KALABSHA ⭐⭐

Built during the great 18th Dynasty (1570–1293 BC) and rebuilt under the Ptolemies and Romans, Kalabsha was dedicated to the Nubian fertility god Marul (the Greeks called him Mandulis). Much of its later decorations have survived. The monuments were relocated here from other sites in Nubia when Lake Nasser was formed and the picturesque Roman Kiosk of Qertassi originally stood 10km away from Kalabsha. More interesting is Beit el Wali (the Governor's House), a small rock-hewn temple built by the Governor of Kush (Ethiopia) during the reign of Ramses II.

➕ 29D2
✉ Next to the High Dam
🕐 Daily 8–4
🚕 Taxi from Aswan. Temple itself can often only be reached by boat from the harbour
👣 Moderate
↔ High Dam (▶ 79)

QASR IBRIM ⭐⭐

Qasr (fortress) Ibrim remains where it was founded in c1000 BC, but what was formerly a mountain top dominating the Nile now only just manages to stay above Lake Nasser. Remains of a healing centre, dedicated to Isis, are visible, as are walls of a 10th-century Christian basilica. From the Ottoman invasion in 1517 until 1812 the castle was manned by Bosnian soldiers.

➕ 29D1
✉ 40km north of Abu Simbel
🕐 Daily 6–6
🚢 Cruise boat only
👣 Free

WADI EL-SEBU'A ⭐⭐

Wadi el-Sebu'a (Valley of the Lions) was named after the 16 sphinxes which line the entrance. The highlights are the many statues and images of Ramses II, in whose reign this was built, and decorations from the time of early Christians, which make for some bizarre contrasts. The Temple of Dakka, reconstructed near by, was begun by Arkamani, a Meroite king contemporary with Ptolemy II (285–246 BC). Dedicated to Thoth, it is the only Egyptian temple facing north. Also here is the Roman temple of Maharraka, dedicated to Isis and Serapis, of which only the Hypostyle Hall survives.

➕ 29D1
✉ 135km south of the High Dam
🕐 Daily 6–6
🚢 Cruise boat only
👣 Free

Suez Canal, Sinai & the Red Sea

The Suez Canal divides Africa from Asia, and Sinai from the rest of Egypt. The desert was too savage for Nile dwellers to settle, but that didn't stop them visiting the mountains on both sides of the divide to find gold (around the Wadi Hammamat), turquoise (at the 12th Dynasty [1990–1780 BC] mines around Serabit el-Khadem) and other minerals. Sinai was always an important transit route and many passed through, from Moses and the Hebrews to Christian hermits living around Wadi Feiran and St Catherine's Monastery, and Muslim pilgrims, thousands of years later, making their way to Mecca. Apart from their traces, the region's main attraction is the sea and what lies beneath it. The days of pristine coastline are long gone, but there are still idyllic places in Sinai and along the Red Sea coast.

> *'At Old Kosseir the sea takes on fabulous colours, with no transition between them – from dark brown to limpid azure. The Red Sea looks more like the ocean than like the Mediterranean. So many shells!'*
>
> GUSTAVE FLAUBERT
> *Carnets de Voyage*
> 25 May 1850

———————•———————

The Gulf of Aqaba with the Saudi Arabian coastline in the far distance

One of many large cruise ships which drop anchor just off Port Said's busy harbourfront on the Suez Canal

Suez Canal

To reach the East from Europe before the 167km-long canal was built meant either sailing around Africa or crossing the desert between Cairo and Suez. When the canal opened in 1869, Suez enjoyed a boom and the new towns of Port Said and Isma'iliya were created. But the Arab-Israel conflict closed the canal, devastated the area (most of Suez was levelled and effectively abandoned between 1967 and 1973) and robbed the area of much of its wealth. Of the three, Port Said has recovered the best, helped by its tax-free status. Since it was nationalised in 1956, the canal has been one of Egypt's major sources of revenue.

What to See in the Suez Canal Area

BUR SA'ID (PORT SAID) ✪

Port Said is no longer 'the wickedest town in the East' – no more dirty postcards or canalside brothels – but it still attracts sailors from around the world. The sights are few: the canal itself – the most captivating thing to see; the plinth at the mouth of the canal where a statue of De Lesseps, the engineer, stood until blown up in 1952; some 19th-century buildings, particularly along the waterfront. The National Museum has a small collection of antiquities and artefacts from the opening of the canal, including Khedive Ismail's carriage.

ISMA'ILIYA ✪

The older, European-built quarter of the city retains its genteel air, typified by the Swiss-style house of Ferdinand de Lesseps, who dreamed and schemed the canal into existence. The dusty museum, built like a Ptolemaic temple, has a small collection of Graeco-Roman and pharaonic artefacts. The city's other main attraction is its beaches, where you can watch freighters pass by.

✚ 29D5
✉ 225km from Cairo, 85km north of Isma'iliya
ℹ Sharia Filastin
☎ 066-235 289
🍴 Cafés/restaurants (£–££)
🚌 Buses from Cairo, Suez, Ismai'liya, Hurghada

National Museum
🕐 Sat–Thu 9–4, Fri 9–11, 1–4

✚ 29D5
✉ 120km east of Cairo, 85km from Port Said
ℹ Mohammed Ali Quay
☎ 064-321 078
🍴 Cafés/restaurants (£–££)
🚌 Buses from Cairo, Hurghada, Port Said

Sinai

Sinai, sitting between Africa and Asia, is a place of rugged landscapes and natural beauty. While most of its coastline is being developed into beach resorts and diving centres, the interior remains a desolate mountain desert with some important Christian holy places and Bedouin communities fighting hard to maintain traditions.

What to See in Sinai

The coast may have been taken over by international tourist resorts but the interior of Sinai is still Bedouin territory

DAHAB ✪

Dahab (Arabic for gold), with its superb beaches and coral reefs, is still considered one of Sinai's best dive sites. The town divides into the Bedouin settlement of el-Asala, the up-market hotels of el-Mashraba and the camps of el-Masbat where backpackers and old hippies hang out. It may be the most relaxed town in Egypt, but beware of bathing topless which is illegal, and of drugs, still widely available although the police are getting tougher. Bedouins organise camel treks into the magnificent desert interior, but Dahab's main sights are undoubtedly under the water, particularly at the Blue Hole and the Canyon (➤ 89).

➕ 29E4
✉ 100km northeast of Sharm el-Sheikh, 570km from Cairo
🍴 Several restaurants in all price categories
🚌 Regular buses from Sharm el-Sheikh, Taba, Nuweiba, Cairo
♿ Few

DEIR SANT KATARIN (ST CATHERINE'S MONASTERY) (➤ 19, TOP TEN)

NUWEIBA ✪

Nuweiba was a thriving resort during the Israeli occupation but now there is little to see or do. The town is divided between the dull port area and the tourist village on a pretty sandy beach. Day-trippers come from Sharm el-Sheikh to swim with a wild dolphin who befriended a local Bedouin. Other Bedouins organise camel treks to the spectacular Coloured Canyon.

➕ 29E4
✉ 72km north of Dahab
🍴 Restaurants (£–£££)
🚌 Regular buses from Cairo, Sharm el-Sheikh, Dahab, Suez and Taba
🛳 At least 1 daily ferry to Aqaba (4hrs) in Jordan

🕂 29E3
✉ 30km from Sharm el-Sheikh
🕐 Sunrise–sunset; camping permits are issued by the visitors' centre
🍴 Restaurant (£–££)
🚕 Taxis or organised tours
💷 Expensive
❓ Passport and visa needed for UN checkpoints

🕂 29E3
✉ 470km from Cairo
🍴 Cafés/restaurants (£–£££)
🚌 Buses from Cairo, Dahab, Nuweiba, Suez and Taba
✈ from Cairo and Luxor
🚢 Ferry from Hurghada several times a week
☎ 069-660 764

🕂 29E4
✉ 390km from Cairo
🚌 Daily buses from Cairo and Sharm el-Sheikh
✈ Flights from Cairo to Ras el-Naqb airport (390km)

RAS MUHAMMAD

Ras Muhammad, Sinai's southernmost tip, was declared Egypt's first national park in 1988. The 12 per cent of the park that can be visited tends to be overwhelmed by day-trippers from Sharm el-Sheikh during high season. Its sandstone mountains, *wadis* (dry gullies) and soft sand dunes are inhabited by foxes, gazelles, ibexes and migratory birds. The stunning coral reefs are a famous haunt for manta rays, sharks and hawksbill turtles, while the magnificent mangroves are breeding grounds for migratory and resident birds.

SHARM EL-SHEIKH

Sharm el-Sheikh was developed, mostly for military purposes, by the Israelis when they occupied Sinai between 1967 and 1982. Over the past few years Sharm has become Egypt's main resort, with many more hotels being built. The Naama Bay area has the highest concentration of hotels and the best facilities for watersports, as well as good snorkelling off the beautiful reef. The only sight is Ras Kennedy, a rock resembling the former US president John F Kennedy's face.

TABA

Taba, a small beach resort on the border with Israel, was returned to Egypt in 1989 after ten years of negotiations. The coastline is beautiful with bays, coves, lagoons and an island. On Geziret el-Faraun (Pharaoh's Island) stands the 12th-century fortress of Salah el-Din, the most important Islamic monument on the Sinai peninsula.

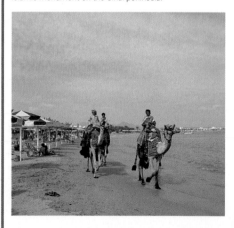

Sun, sea, sand – and a touch of the Orient on the beach at Sharm el-Sheikh

Top Red Sea Diving & Snorkelling Sites

Sinai

On-line information
www.redseaexperience.com
www.red-sea.com

- **Blue Hole** (a few kilometres north of Dahab). Pleasant, easy diving and snorkelling on the outer reef of the Blue Hole lagoon, with mainly hard corals and a large variety of reef fish.
- **The Canyon** (on the way to the Blue Hole, Dahab). A long, narrow and very beautiful canyon, with plenty to see even for inexperienced divers.
- **The Islands** (near Laguna Hotel, Dahab). Spectacular labyrinth of coral peaks, bowls and corridors, teeming with fish and the occasional turtle.
- **End of the Road Reef** (extreme end of Nabq coastal road, north of Sharm el-Sheikh). Submerged island with some of the best corals in Egypt. Abundant fish life.
- **Shark Observatory** (Ras Muhammad). A vertical wall of soft and hard coral which attracts barracuda, grey and blacktip sharks and Napoleon fish.
- **Ras Ghozlani** (Ras Muhammad). Nicest spot on the southern coast to observe the abundant small reef species and well-preserved corals.

A diver meets a scary looking Crown of Thorns

Red Sea Coast

- **Carless (Careless) Reef** (5km north of Giftun Island). Famous for its semi-tame moray eels, but untamed sharks and jacks can often be spotted.
- **Green Hole** (59km north of Quseir). Magnificent coral growth, dolphins and blue-eagle rays as well as the usual reef species.
- **Beit Goha** (20km north of Quseir). Exceptional, very shallow, coral garden, still in great condition, with sturgeon fish, grouper, trumpet fish and many others.
- **Sirena Beach Home Reef** (in front of Mövenpick Hotel, Quseir). Just off the jetty is a reef with a huge variety of both corals and fish, including giant schools of tuna, Napoleon and lion fish.

The Red Sea coast as it used to look, but now rarely does, as a line of tourist resorts is being planned from Suez down to the Sudanese border

Red Sea Coast

Ancient Egyptians looked for gold, copper and precious stones in the Red Sea mountains, while early Coptic saints Anthony and Paul took refuge here from Roman persecutors and in due course founded the world's first monasteries. Today much of the 1,600km of coast from Suez to the border of Sudan, with its beautiful sandy coves and magnificent coral reefs, is being developed into beach resorts and its fragile habitat is increasingly coming under threat.

What to See on the Red Sea Coast

EL-GHARDAQA (HURGHADA)

Hurghada has developed fast, some say too fast, from a tiny fishing village into one of Egypt's most popular destinations. The town and its tourist bazaar are of little interest, but large beach resorts offering a variety of watersports make up for that. The water is warm for much of the year and there is a cooling breeze in the hot summers. For those not into diving or snorkelling there is the Sindbad Submarine (► 110), a small Red Sea Aquarium (► 110) or the Aquascope at the Royal Palace hotel (☎ 065-443 710).

EL-GOUNA

Self-contained up-market resort with several hotels, a residential area with holiday homes for wealthy Cairenes, an 18-hole golf course and several very pleasant lagoons. El-Gouna has its own airport, an aquarium and a small museum with good replicas of ancient Egyptian treasures.

EL-QUSEYR (QUSEIR)

Until the 10th century the largest port on the Red Sea, the sleepy town of Quseir, overlooked by a 16th-century fort, offers a welcome alternative to the crowds of Hurghada. There is wonderful snorkelling off the beaches and this is a good base from which to explore the deep south.

EL-GHARDAQA (HURGHADA)

✪ 29D3
✉ 529km southeast of Cairo
ℹ On Resort Strip
☎ 065-444 420
🍴 Restaurants (£–£££)
🚌 Daily buses from Cairo, Luxor, Aswan and Suez
✈ Flights from Cairo, Luxor, Sharm el-Sheikh
⛴ Ferry to Sharm el-Sheikh (☎ 065-545 147)

EL-GOUNA

✪ 29D3
✉ 30km north of Hurghada
🍴 Restaurants (£–£££)
🚌 Taxis from Hurghada
✈ Flights from Cairo
☎ 065-547 934

EL-QUSEYR (QUSEIR)

✪ 29E3
✉ 80km south of Hurghada
🍴 Hotel restaurants (££–£££)
🚌 Buses from Cairo, Marsa Alam and Hurghada

Where To...

Eat and Drink	92–99
Stay	100–05
Shop	106–09
Take the Children	110–11
Be Entertained	112–16

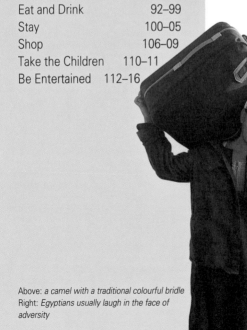

Above: *a camel with a traditional colourful bridle*
Right: *Egyptians usually laugh in the face of adversity*

91

Cairo & Environs

Price categories
Prices are for a three-course meal for two without drinks or service.

£ = less than 100LE
££ = 100–200LE
£££ = more than 200LE

Abu el-Sid (££–£££)
Egyptian restaurant in an old building with traditional Louis Farouk-style furniture and work by local artists on the wall. Traditional dishes are served with style and water pipes for those who want. Incredibly busy and trendy, so book well in advance.
✉ 157 Sharia 26th-of-July, Zamalek ☎ 02-735 9640
🕐 11AM–4AM

Abu Shaqra (£–££)
Known as the 'King of Kebab' this is one of the best places in Cairo to eat a simple and plain kebab.
✉ 69 Sharia Qasr el-Aini, Garden City ☎ 02-531 6111
🕐 Noon–2AM

After Eight (££)
Not easy to find down a small alley, but worth looking for, particularly at night when there is live jazz. The menu includes simple Western and well-prepared Middle Eastern specialities.
✉ 6 Sharia Qasr an-Nil ☎ 02-574 0855 🕐 Lunch, dinner

Alfi Bey (£–££)
Simple Egyptian cooking is served with a smile at this atmospheric old-fashioned restaurant. Start with *mezze* (appertisers), followed by pigeons stuffed with *firik* (crushed wheat) or a lamb kebab, and finish with rice pudding or *mahallabiya* (dessert made of rice flour). No alcohol.
✉ 3 Sharia Alfi, Downtown
☎ 02-577 4999 🕐 1PM–1AM

Americana Fish Market (££)
A spacious boat moored on the Nile where you can choose your fresh fish or seafood from the display, then tell the chef how you would like it cooked. Salads are equally well prepared and be sure to try a dessert from the trolley.
✉ 26 Sharia el-Nil, Giza
☎ 02-570 9693
🕐 12:30PM–2:30AM

Andrea (£–££)
Delightful garden restaurant, with an indoor room for the evenings and cold days. Excellent roasted chicken and grills with Oriental salads and freshly baked *baladi* bread. Children's play area in the garden.
✉ 59–60 Marioutiya Canal, El-Ahram, Giza ☎ 02-383 1133
🕐 Noon–1AM

Arabesque (££)
Old-fashioned Levantine restaurant with faded Moorish interior and sometimes variable cuisine, tucked away behind an art gallery. French dishes are good here, but try the *meloukhiya* with chicken or rabbit, pigeon with Oriental rice and one of the best *Umm Ali's* (milky bread pudding with coconut, raisins and cream) in town.
✉ 6 Sharia Qasr el-Nil, Downtown ☎ 02-574 7898
🕐 Lunch, dinner

Bird Cage (££–£££)
Excellent Thai restaurant serving well prepared and beautifully presented dishes including deep-fried prawns in *konafa* (angel hair) and delicious spicy curries. The service is swift and the ambience very pleasant.
✉ Semiramis Inter Continental, Corniche el-Nil Garden City ☎ 02-795 7171
🕐 12:30–4, 7–12

La Bodega (££–£££)

Trendy bistro with Mediterranean specialities from Algerian couscous to ravioli and everything between. The lounge is more upmarket serving excellent fusion dishes in a minimal Asian decor, to a Buddha Bar beat.

✉ 157 26th-of-July Street, Zamalek ☎ 02-735 6761 🕐 12–2, 7–4

Café Riche (£–££)

Riche oozes history, as the place where the famous Umm Kulthoum started her career, and where Gamal Abdel Nasser planned the revolution. The food is simple and fresh, but don't expect grand cuisine – stick to soups, salads and sandwiches.

✉ 17 Sharia Talaat Harb, Downtown ☎ 02-392 9793 🕐 9:30AM–1AM

Cilantro (£–££)

Stylish café that serves good coffee with fresh croissants for breakfast, healthy sandwiches and delicious fresh juices.

✉ 31 Sharia Mohammed Mahmoud, opp AUC, Downtown ☎ 02-792 4571 🕐 9AM–2AM

Egyptian Pancake House (£)

Delicious sweet and savoury *fateers*, a cross between a pancake and a pizza.

✉ Between Sharia el-Azhar and Midan el-Husayn, Khan el-Khalili 🕐 All day

Felfela (£)

The original of a growing chain which offers a good introduction to traditional Egyptian cuisine in kitsch and exotic surroundings. A large selection of salads, *fuul* (fava bean) dishes and grilled meats at reasonable prices.

✉ 15 Sharia Hoda Shaarawi, Downtown ☎ 02-392 2833 🕐 8:30AM–1:30AM

El-Fishawi (£)

The oldest teahouse in Cairo, claiming never to have closed since 1773. A great place to sip tea, smoke a waterpipe and watch the world go by. No alcohol.

✉ Just off Midan el-Husayn, Khan el-Khalili 🕐 24 hours

Moghul Room (£££)

A good place to recover from a hectic day, this elegant and beautifully decorated restaurant serves authentic Indian food, with soothing live Indian music every night.

✉ Mena House Oberoi Hotel, Sharia el-Ahram, near the Giza Pyramids ☎ 02-383 3222/3444 🕐 Lunch, dinner

El-Morocco (££–£££)

Fashionable Moroccan restaurant on an old cruise boat. The decor is sumptuous, service impeccable and the Moroccan cuisine is delicious. Later in the night the music is turned up and the place becomes a trendy nightspot.

✉ 9 Saraya el-Gezira Street, Zamalek ☎ 02-735 3314 🕐 8:30PM–1AM

Greek Club (£–££)

The old Greek club with lots of faded grandeur and a large breezy terrace, is the perfect place for cool beer on a sweltering hot Cairene night. The food is nothing special, but it is edible.

✉ Above Groppi on Sharia Qasr el-Nil, Downtown ☎ 02-574 0855 🕐 12–3, 8–2

Jo Sushi (££)

Small Asian restaurant that does a good sushi or Californian roll, and for those not keen on raw fish there is a small selection of Chinese dishes and Japanese stews. Friendly atmosphere and good service.

✉ 47 Sharia Mohammed Mazhar, Zamalek ☎ 02-735 7746 🕐 Noon–midnight

A Waterpipe and Mint Tea

On a hot balmy Cairene evening, after dinner in one of the city's many restaurants, head for the cafés around Midan el-Husayn. The area is very lively until after midnight, and packed during religious festivals (► 116). The many cafés, including El-Fishawi and El-Sukkariya, serve fresh fruit juices, herbal teas, coffee and a digestive mint tea. Egyptians love to watch the world go by whilst smoking a *sheesha* (waterpipe) with *tumbac* (tobacco), *maassal* (tobacco with molasses) or *tuffah* (tobacco sweetened with apple), and you shouldn't leave the country without trying it.

93

Juice bars

One of the pleasures of Egypt are the colourful tiled juice bars with pyramids of oranges, strawberries and guavas announcing their trade. Juices are cheap and usually freshly squeezed on the spot. Try whatever is in season: sweet sugarcane, orange, carrot, delicious mango, pomegranate, guava or strawberry, or the local version of a milkshake, milk with bananas.

Justine (£££)

Zamalek's most formal and best French restaurant. The service is great and the food classic and excellent. Part of the Four Corners restaurant complex that also includes the popular Italian restaurant La Piazza.

✉ Four Corners, 4 Sharia Hassan Sabri, Zamalek ☎ 02-736 2961 🕐 12:30–3, 8–11

Naguib Mahfouz Coffee Shop (£) & Khan el-Khalili Restaurant (££)

The only up-market place to eat in the bazaar (as well as the only decent toilets) with traditional Egyptian drinks, waterpipes and sweets in the coffee shop and *mezze* (appetisers) and traditional dishes in the restaurant. Mainly for tourists, but a cosy and quiet place to retire from the busy streets.

✉ 5 el-Badestan alley, Khan el-Khalili ☎ 02-590 3788 🕐 11AM–midnight

Paradise Island (££)

This floating terrace with a wide view over the Nile is the perfect place for an evening drink, waterpipe or table of *mezze*.

✉ Gezira Sheraton. 3 Sharia Magles Qa'det el-Thawra, Gezira ☎ 02-737 3737 🕐 5PM–1AM

Peking (££)

Freshly prepared and reasonably authentic Cantonese food, in a perhaps less authentic but rather quirky Chinese setting. Popular choice with those wanting something different than *mezze*.

✉ 14 Sharia Saraya el-Ezbekiya, behind Cinema Diana, Downtown ☎ 02-591 2381 🕐 Noon–1AM

Revolving Restaurant (£££)

Located on the 41st floor, this is undoubtedly the restaurant with the best view, and the food is superb, too. Set around the show kitchen where you can see the chefs whip up culinary delights from all over the world. Formal dress. Book in advance.

✉ Grand Hyatt Hotel, on the Corniche, Garden City ☎ 02-365 1234 🕐 7PM–last orders

Sabaya (££–£££)

The best Lebanese restaurant in town with a great variety of *mezze*, including several different *kibbeh nayyeh* (raw pounded lamb). Peaceful, modern Oriental decor and extremely good service from the truly delightful waiters.

✉ Semiramis Inter Continental, Corniche el-Nil Garden City ☎ 02-795 7171 🕐 12:30–4, 7–12

Samakmak (££)

No menu, just select your fish from the catch of the day, have it fried or grilled, and it will be served with rice, bread and salads. After a delicious meal, have a waterpipe while overlooking Cairo traffic.

✉ 92 Sharia Ahmed Orabi, Mohandiseen ☎ 02-302 7308 🕐 Noon–4AM

Seasons (£££)

One of the best restaurants in the area, set in an elegant interior that reminds more of Manhattan than Cairo, but then the Nile is just there outside. The eclectic menu offers superb food that is beautifully presented. Excellent service too.

✉ Four Seasons Hotel, 35 Giza Street ☎ 02-573 1212 🕐 7AM–1:30AM

Simmonds Coffee Shop (£)

Good place for a breakfast pastry at the bar, washed down with fresh fruit juice and for coffee all day.

✉ 112 Sharia 26 July, Zamalek 🕐 All day

Alexandria & the Oases

Alexandria

Cap d'Or (£–££)
This atmospheric bar-restaurant is one of the few remaining reminders of Alexandria's old Greek tavernas. Try the calamari stew with a cool beer, while listening to 1970s French *chanson* or watching local *habitués* shooting the breeze.
✉ 4 Sharia Adib, off Sharia Saad Zagloul ☷ Noon–2AM

Elite (£–££)
A simple whitewashed cafeteria-restaurant that has seen better days, but still retains a Mediterranean air different than the buzz in the shopping street outside. Madame Christina has been running the place for decades and still reigns supreme.
✉ 43 Sharia Safiya Zaghloul
☎ 03-486 3592
☷ 9AM–midnight

Fish Market (££–£££)
An up-market fish restaurant with excellent fish, good service and sweeping views of the bay and harbour.
✉ El-Kashafa el-Bahariya Club, 26 Corniche el-Nil ☎ 03-480 5119 ☷ Lunch, dinner

Samakmak (££)
Near the fish market, this unpretentious restaurant is what you'd expect a fish restaurant to be. There is indoor and outdoor seating, and the very fresh fish you choose from the counter is grilled or fried as you wish.
✉ 42 Qasr Ras et-Tin, Bahari
☎ 03-481 1560
☷ Lunch, dinner

Spitfire Bar (£)
Popular 1970s bar, playing good old rock 'n' roll and filled to the brim with memorabilia and pictures from loyal customers, including American sailors, many of whom like to drop in when at anchor.
✉ 7 Sharia el-Bursa el-Qadima ☎ 03-480 6503
☷ Noon–1AM (or later)

Splash (££)
This relaxed Italian restaurant in the heart of the trendy shopping mall is the place of the moment. The menu is a creative mix of old and new style Italian cuisine, but make sure you keep a space for the tempting desserts.
✉ Hilton Alexandria Green Plaza, Smouha ☎ 03-420 9120
☷ 1–4, 6:30–11

The Oases

Kenooz (£–££)
Delightful Siwan restaurant, serving simple well-prepared Egyptian dishes in the welcome shade of palm trees. If it's too hot to eat, fall back on the matresses on the terrace for a good waterpipe with fresh lemon juice.
✉ Sharia Subukha, Siwa Town
☎ 046-460 1299
☷ 9AM–midnight

Popular Restaurant (£)
Known as Bayyoumi's, this good eatery serves meat and vegetable stews, bread, omelettes and soup, but check the price first.
✉ At the main intersection of el-Bawiti, Bahariya
☷ Breakfast, lunch, dinner

Restaurant of El Badawiyya Hotel (£–££)
Excellent restaurant with well-prepared, freshly cooked Egyptian food served in a courtyard.
✉ Farafra ☎ 092-510 060
☷ All day

Alexandria's Patisseries
One of the best places to look for 'Old Alexandria' is in its many old-fashioned patisseries. Try Athineos at 21 Midan Saad Zaghloul; Trianon at Midan Zaghloul; the pleasant garden at Baudrot, 23 Sharia Saad Zaghloul; the elegant sugary decor at Venous, 12 Sharia el-Hurriya.

Nile Valley & Nubia

Karkadeh
Many hotels in Upper Egypt offer a glass of sweet *karkadeh* as a welcome drink. This delicious dark red infusion of dried hibiscus flowers can be drunk hot in winter, but is usually served ice-cold. It is also used in cocktails mixed with gin or vodka. Dried hibiscus flowers are cheap and can be bought anywhere in Egypt, but are particularly good in the *souk* in Aswan.

Aswan
Aswan Moon (£)
Popular Nile-side restaurant with a mock castle entrance and a terrace on a floating pontoon. The food is fine, especially the Egyptian *mezze* (appetisers) and stews, and the fresh fruit juices are a treat, but it's the ambience most people come for. This is the meeting place for young Aswanis in search of beer, felucca captains singing Nubian songs and tourists enjoying views of the river or trying to organise a boat trip.
✉ **Corniche el-Nil** ☎ **097-316 108** ⏰ **Lunch, dinner**

Aswan Panorama (£)
Waterfront café-restaurant serving simple Egyptian *mezze* (appetisers) and other dishes, as well as drinks and fresh juices. For those who want something quieter than the lively atmosphere at the Aswan Moon.
✉ **Corniche el-Nil, beside the Aswan Moon** ☎ **097-316 169** ⏰ **All day**

Darna (££)
Pleasant restaurant designed as an Egyptian house serving a buffet with traditional dishes. One of the few places in Aswan with a good selection.
✉ **New Cataract Hotel, Sharia Abtal el-Tahrir** ☎ **097-316 002** ⏰ **Dinner only**

Al-Misri Tour Restaurant (£)
With a men-only room in the front and family room at the back, this rather quaint but very clean place serves some of the best *koftas* and kebabs in town, so it can be hard to get a seat.
✉ **Sharia el-Matar, off Sharia el-Suq; ask for directions, as everyone knows it** ☎ **097-302 576** ⏰ **All day**

1902 Restaurant (£££)
Ok French and international cuisine is served in this elegant, turn-of-the-century Moorish dining hall. Nubian dancers and musicians add spice to the experience.
✉ **Old Cataract Hotel, Sharia Abtal el-Tahrir** ☎ **097-316 000** ⏰ **Dinner only**

Nubian House (££)
The setting of this Nubian-style house on a cliff overlooking the Nile is stunning, and the Egyptian-Nubian food is good. The restaurant also offers tea while you watch the sunset from the terrace. Live Nubian music at night.
✉ **On the river, 700m beyond the Nubia Museum** ☎ **097-326 226** ⏰ **Noon–midnight**

Old Cataract Terrace (££)
This splendid hotel terrace for tea or at sunset has become one of the sights. The view is spectacular and Earl Grey tea with cakes and sandwiches is a treat, but beware that there is a steep minimum charge for non-residents from 4PM to sunset.
✉ **Old Cataract Hotel, Sharia Abtal el-Tahrir** ☎ **097-316 000** ⏰ **All day**

Luxor
Al-Moudira (££–£££)
The best restaurant in town, either indoors or outdoors by the pool, serves excellent Lebanese and Mediterranean food.
✉ **10km south of the Valley of the Queens, Daba'iyya** ☎ **012-325 1307** ⏰ **Lunch, dinner**

Restaurant Mohamed (£)
Simple restaurant in a West Bank house where you can sample real Egyptian food. Small menu, but give Mohamed some warning and he will prepare a delicious *meloukhiya* (vegetable soup), stuffed pigeon or grilled kebabs, all served with cold beer.

✉ Next to the Pharaoh's Hotel, West Bank ☎ 095-311 014 🕐 Lunch, dinner

Jamboree Restaurant (££)
Behind the Mena Palace Hotel, with British owners, and serving both Egyptian and international food on its roof terrace .

✉ 1712 Sharia al-Montazah ☎ 010-146 1712

King's Head Pub (£–££)
A British pub with all the trimmings: darts, pub food, billiards, football on TV and lots of British tourists happy to have found a home away from home.

✉ Sharia Khaled Ibn el-Walid ☎ 095-371 249 🕐 24 hours

La Mamma (££)
An Italian restaurant set in a pleasant garden with a pond full of wading birds. The fresh pastas and meat dishes are good.

✉ Sheraton Hotel, Sharia Khalid Ibn Walid ☎ 095-374 544 🕐 Lunch, dinner

Maratonga Café-Restaurant (£)
This lovely shady terrace is a good place to stop for lunch or, after a long day of sightseeing, to see the late afternoon sun shine orange on the magnificent temple. You can either stop for a drink or try the simple but well-prepared Egyptian dishes.

✉ Opposite Madinat Habu Temple 🕐 All day

Marsam Hotel Restaurant (£)
The food is cheap and tasty, mainly Egyptian fare, and there is a good chance that you'll run into some of the archaeologists excavating in the neigbourhood. Best in spring and autumn. No beer.

✉ Opposite the Valley of the Nobles, West Bank ☎ 095-382 403 🕐 Lunch, dinner

Mövenpick Restaurants (££–£££)
Good fresh food such as salads, pizzas and kebabs are served on the terrace by day, with views over the Nile and the green bank on the other side. At night there is an indoor buffet or à la carte menu. Swiss ice-creams are a speciality.

✉ Crocodile Island, 5km from Luxor Centre ☎ 095-374 855 🕐 Lunch, dinner

Royal Bar (£)
Old-fashioned colonial bar, perfect for an early evening aperitif or beer, or try the hotel's elegant terrace to watch the sunset.

✉ Old Winter Palace, Corniche el-Nil ☎ 095-380 422 🕐 Afternoons and evenings

Tutankhamun (£)
Tutankhamun is by far the best on this strip. The chef and owner used to cook in one of Luxor's five star hotels. Chicken with rosemary, served with sweet Oriental rice, is a speciality.

✉ Near the public ferry landing on the West Bank ☎ 095-310 118 🕐 Lunch, dinner

Food Markets
The best place to buy fresh produce for a picnic or a long-distance felucca trip is the market. In Luxor, beyond the tourist *souk* on Sharia el-Birka, there are a few fruit and vegetable stalls as well as groceries. On Tuesdays there is also a fruit and vegetable market on Sharia Television, Luxor. In Aswan head for Sharia el-Souk, near the station.

Suez Canal, Sinai & the Red Sea

Cruise the Suez Canal

For the best view of the Suez Canal, try a lunch or dinner cruise. Nora's Floating Restaurant (☎ 066 326 804, check for exact departure times) offers cruises with good Egyptian food and great views, departing from Sharia Filastin in Port Said, opposite the National Museum.

Suez Zone

Galal Seafood (£–££)

This cheap seafood restaurant is a local favourite. Galal serves fresh calamari, shrimps and fish as well as Greek-style *mezze*. Beer is served inside, but not on the very pleasant terrace.

✉ **Sharia el-Gumhureyya, Port Said** ☎ **066-229 668**
🕔 **Lunch, dinner**

George's (££)

Cairenes come for the day to sample George's famously fresh seafood and fish. Little has changed in this Greek-run restaurant since 1950.

✉ **Sharia Sultan Hussein, Isma'iliya** ☎ **064-917 327**
🕔 **Lunch, dinner**

Sinai

Sharm el-Sheikh

Bus Stop (££)

Trendiest place in town, with a façade and interior shaped like a bus. Sounds tacky but it is actually quite fun, and the place turns into a discothèque later at night. The rooftop bar in the Sanafir is the other place to be seen, especially earlier in the evening.

✉ **Sanafir Hotel, Naama Bay** ☎ **062-600 197**
🕔 **7PM–6AM**

Al-Fanar (££)

The name means lighthouse and that is where this open-air Bedouin-style restaurant is located, at the foot of Sharm's lighthouse. Good Italian food and excellent sea views.

✉ **Ras Um Sid** ☎ **062-622 218**

Hard Rock Café (£–££)

Casual atmosphere and the usual memorabilia which belonged to rock stars such as Madonna, Elton John and Elvis Presley. (Late night discos.)

✉ **Naama Bay** ☎ **062-602 665**
🕔 **12:30PM–2AM (4AM at weekends)**

Fish Restaurant (£££)

Quiet outdoor fish restaurant, decorated with fishing nets and other fishing paraphernalia, serving excellent French fish and seafood dishes. Service can be erratic.

✉ **Near diving centre, Hilton Fayrouz, Naama Bay** ☎ **062-660 136** 🕔 **Dinner only**

Pirates Bar (££)

Popular venue for an evening drink, in a romantic garden with bridges over little ponds. Happy hour 5:30–7:30.

✉ **Hilton Fayrouz, Naama Bay** ☎ **062-600 140** 🕔 **Evening**

La Rustichella (££)

One of the best Italian restaurants in town, very popular with the large Italian contingent, serving Italian food as only 'la mamma' can cook it. Great choice of pastas. Book in advance.

✉ **Behind Na'ama Bay** ☎ **010-116 0692** 🕔 **Lunch, dinner**

Sala Thai (££–£££)

Excellent Thai restaurant with a modern Asian decor and a lovely terrace overlooking the sea.

✉ **Hyatt Regency Hotel, Na'ama Bay** ☎ **069-601 234**
🕔 **Dinner**

TamTam (£–££)

Large menu with simple but excellent Egyptian food

served in this popular indoor restaurant or on the more pleasant terrace.

✉ **Ghazala Hotel, Naama Bay** ☎ **062-600 150/9** ⏰ **Lunch, dinner**

Red Sea

El-Ghardaqa (Hurghada)
Chill (££)

The hottest place in town, this totally relaxed beach restaurant with bar serves great Mediterranean food with a slightly changed menu every day.

✉ **Sharia Sheraton, Sigala** ☎ **012-382 0694** ⏰ **11AM–1AM**

Felfela (£–££)

Branch of the popular Cairene chain (► 92–93) serving good and reasonably priced Egyptian fare.

✉ **Sharia Sheraton** ☎ **065-442 410** ⏰ **Lunch, dinner**

Italian Restaurant (££–£££)

Delicious and inventive Italian dishes, home-made pastas and tender *involtini* (stuffed veal rolls), served on a romantic garden terrace.

✉ **Intercontinental Hurghada Hotel** ☎ **065-446 911** ⏰ **Dinner**

Joker (££)

Very popular fish restaurant with a wide choice of the freshest fish and seafood, you can choose by the weight, all served with *mezze* and bread. No alcohol.

✉ **Midan Sigala** ☎ **065-543 146** ⏰ **Lunch, dinner**

Lo Scarabeo (££)

Great Italian restaurant with the usual pizzas and pastas, run and mostly frequented by Italians. A nice terrace in the evening.

✉ **Sharia Sayyed el-Qorayem, el-Dahar** ☎ **012-364 6927** ⏰ **Lunch, dinner**

Portofino (££)

Italian fish and seafood specialities as well as fresh home-made pasta are served in this pleasant Italian restaurant.

✉ **Sharia Sayyed el-Qorayem, el-Dahar** ☎ **065-546 250** ⏰ **Lunch, dinner**

El-Gouna
Kiki's Italian Cuisine (££)

Popular restaurant with two open-air terraces offering great views over the town and lagoons. The food is excellent with fresh home-made pastas and salads.

✉ **Above the museum in Kafr el-Gouna** ☎ **065-542 407** ⏰ **Dinner**

Sayyadin Fish Restaurant (££)

Airy and spacious fish restaurant on the beach with a large terrace, serving excellent fish and seafood.

✉ **Mövenpick Hotel, on the beach** ☎ **065-545 160** ⏰ **Lunch, dinner**

Le Tabasco (££)

Branch of the funky Cairene bar-restaurant with excellent Mediterranean food, great music and a very trendy modern Egyptian interior.

✉ **Near the museum, Kafr el-Gouna** ☎ **065-545 516** ⏰ **Lunch, dinner**

El-Tayibeen Café (£)

Relaxed and laid-back Egyptian-style café with sweets, tea and waterpipes.

✉ **Kafr el-Gouna** ☎ **065-542 460** ⏰ **All day**

Fuul, Fuul, Fuul

One of Egypt's most popular dishes is undoubtedly *fuul*, or fava beans, stewed in water for 12 hours. Cheap and wholesome, often eaten for breakfast, it is a favourite at all levels of Egyptian society. Everyone has their own trick to customise this earthy brown stew – try it with lemon and cumin, green pepper, egg, oil or tomatoes. There is a superstition that eating too much *fuul* is bad for the brain and the diet of *fuul* is often cited as the cause of the nation's woes, from the lethargy of bureaucrats to the crazy driving in Cairo's streets.

Cairo

Hotel prices
Prices are for a double room with bathroom

£   = less than US$30
££   = US$30–100
£££ = over US$100

Cairo Marriott (£££)

Khedive Ismail's sumptuous palace on the Nile, built for the celebrations marking the opening of the Suez Canal in 1869, has been turned into the central area of the Marriott Hotel. Rooms in the two modern towers lack atmosphere but have splendid views over the Nile and city. The bedroom of the French empress Eugenie is now Eugenie's Lounge, an elegant cocktail bar, and there is a swimming pool in the Khedival gardens. The garden Promenade is a popular terrace café.

✉ Sharia Saray el-Gezira, Zamalek ☎ 02-735 8888; reservation@cairomarriott.com

Carlton (££)

This 1950s very central hotel has changed little over the years and it is a great one for those who like faded grandeur. The rooms vary a lot in size and light, so check first before you take the room. Good value.

✉ 21 Sharia 26th of July, Downtown ☎ 02-575 2323; carlton@menanet.net

Cosmopolitan (££)

This magnificent art nouveau building is right in the centre but in a surprisingly quiet back street. Spacious and comfortable rooms.

✉ 1 Sharia Ibn Tahlab, Downtown ☎ 02-392 3845, fax 02-393 3531

Four Seasons (£££)

Beautifully re-created classical-style hotel overlooking the zoological and botanical gardens with views of the Nile and distant pyramids. Marble bathrooms and spa/health centre.

✉ 35 Sharia el-Giza, Giza ☎ 02-573 1212, fax 02-568 1616; www.fourseasons.com

Golden Tulip Flamenco (££)

Modern hotel in a residential area at the back of the island of Zamalek, close to shops and restaurants, with clean, cosy rooms. Some rooms overlook the Nile and even have views of the Giza pyramids on a clear day. Good Spanish restaurant.

✉ 2 Sharia el-Gezira el-Wusta, Zamalek ☎ 02-735 0815; www.flamencohotels.com

Horus House (££)

Very quiet hotel in residential area, often booked in advance by regular visitors who like its friendly, homely atmosphere. The restaurant offers a good-value lunch, and has amongst its regulars some older couples who live on the island.

✉ 21 Sharia Ismail Muhamad, Zamalek ☎ 02-735 3634, fax 02-735 3182

Ismailiya House (£)

A backpackers' haven with clean, cheerful rooms and dormitories, MTV and an excellent laundry service, overlooking the square (noisy) or Downtown Cairo. Book well in advance.

✉ 7th floor, 1 Midan Tahrir, Downtown ☎ 02-796 3122, ismahouse@hotmail.com

Lialy Hostel (£)

A recent arrival on the budget scene, the Lialy has very clean and spacious rooms on this busy but very central square. The staff are very friendly and helpful, and there is an internet café attached.

✉ 3rd floor, Midan Talaat Harb, Downtown ☎ 02-575 2802; www.hostelworld.com

Mayfair (£)
Small quiet hotel in a tree-lined street with spotless rooms, some with a balcony overlooking the street. Tranquil terrace for having an afternoon drink.
✉ 9 Sharia Aziz Osman, Zamalek ☎ 02-735 7315; www.mayfaircairo.com

Mena House Oberoi (£££)
Rooms in the more expensive 19th-century wing of this former Khedival hunting lodge are stylish and beautifully decorated. Some have views over the pyramids. Most rooms are in the modern garden annexe that is less characterful but has similar views. The Moghul Room (➤ 93) is considered the best Indian restaurant in Cairo, while at the Rubayyat nightclub some of the best belly dancers perform.
✉ Sharia el-Ahram, Giza ☎ 02-383 3222, fax 02-383 7777; www.oberoihotels.com

Meramees (£)
Small but very popular budget hotel in the centre of Cairo owned by the extremely friendly Mamdouh Mohammed who knows a lot about Cairo. Spotless and comfortable rooms as well as dormitories.
✉ 32 Sharia Sabry Abu Alam, Downtown ☎ 02-396 2318, meramees_hotel@hotmail.com

Nile Hilton (£££)
One of Egypt's first modern international hotels with an authentic ancient statue in its lobby. The comfortable rooms either overlook the Nile or Downtown Cairo, and the bars and restaurants are popular meeting places.
✉ Corniche el-Nil/Tahrir Square ☎ 02-578 0444; www.hilton.com

Pension Roma (£)
An old-style 1940s hotel with clean rooms, polished wooden floors and nice old furniture. Very popular, so it is advisable to book ahead.
✉ 169 Sharia Muhamad Farid, 6th floor ☎ 02-391 1088; fax 02-579 6243

Saqqara Country Club and Hotel (££)
Tranquil hotel in the green Saqqara countryside, with horse-riding facilities. Day membership to the country club is available.
✉ Saqqara Road to Abu el-Nomros ☎ 02-384 6115, fax 02-385 0577

Semiramis InterContinental (£££)
Centrally located Semiramis has five-star amenities and spacious rooms, most with great views over the Nile. The excellent restaurants include the French restaurant Le Grill, Sabaya and Bird Cage (➤ 93).
✉ Corniche en-Nil, Downtown ☎ 02-795 7171; www.cairo.intercontinental.com

Victoria (££)
Near Ramses station, this noisy, characterful 1940s hotel has spacious, spotless rooms with mahogany furniture and air-conditioning. Delightful little café-terrace in the garden.
✉ 66 Sharia Gumhuriya, Downtown ☎ 02-589 2290, fax 02-591 3008

Windsor (£–££)
Well-run budget hotel, considered Downtown's best, in a Moorish-style building with clean spacious rooms, arched windows and high ceilings. Delightful colonial-style bar on the first floor, totally musty and old-fashioned. Book in advance.
✉ 19 Sharia el-Alfi, Downtown ☎ 02-591 5277, fax 02-592 1621; www.windsorcairo.com

A Hotel Like No Other
The El-Hussein Hotel at Midan el-Husayn, Islamic Cairo ☎ 02-591 8089 is rather run down but uniquely situated in the heart of the Islamic city, with balconies overlooking the busy square outside the mosque of Husayn. Don't hope to sleep during festival times. In spite of the loud noise from *muezzin* calling for prayers five times a day and wedding parties celebrating all night long, the atmosphere is great. Try the roof terrace for a drink and to see the sun set over the old city's domes, minarets and TV antennae.

Alexandria & the Oases

Ecology in the Oases

Tours of the Western Desert oases are becoming increasingly popular, but the fragile desert environment is already showing the strain. Basic environmentally friendly practices such as taking all rubbish away with you and burning all toilet paper seem obvious but are not always observed. Many antiquities here are under threat as some guides show more concern for profit and self-promotion, helping tourists to take away antiquities, inscribe their names on the rocks or spray water on prehistoric rock paintings to get better pictures. For recommended desert guides ➤ 114.

Alexandria

Cecil (££)

This famous and once grand hotel has been stripped of much of its character over the years, and now is only a shadow of its former self. The rooms are fine though, the views over the Med are great and it is very central.

✉ Midan Saad Zaghloul
☎ 03-487 7173, fax 03-485 5655

Metropole (££)

Period hotel with charming high-ceilinged rooms and lots of atmosphere. Excellent and friendly service. Serious competition for the neighbouring Cecil. Reserve ahead.

✉ 52 Sharia Saad Zaghloul
☎ 03-484 0910

Salamlek Palace (£££)

Next door to the presidential summer palace, this former hunting lodge has been turned into a luxurious hotel. The rooms are over the top period-style luxury and the hotel has a casino and some good restaurants. Set in the Montazah gardens a long way from the major sights.

✉ Montazah Gardens
☎ 03-547 7999, fax 03-547 3585

Union (£)

Probably the best budget option in Alexandria, with very clean and comfortable rooms, some with superb views over the Eastern Harbour.

✉ 164 Sharia 26th of July
☎ 03-480 7312

Oases

Adrere Amellal (£££)

Delightful desert eco-lodge set in its own oasis at the edge of the salt lake. Every room is different, built in the traditional mud and salt, lit by candlelight and the pool flows out of a Roman spring. The delicious food from the organic garden is served on old family china.

✉ Sidi Jaafar, outside Siwa Town ☎ 02-736 7879; info@eqi.come.eg

El-Beshmo Lodge (£)

A most pleasant hotel on the edge of a palm grove opposite the Roman hot spring of the same name. Simple but spotless comfortable rooms with private or shared bathrooms.

✉ 10-minute walk from main street, el-Bawiti, Bahariya
☎ & fax 02-847 2177

El Badawiyya Safari and Hotel (£)

One of the best hotels in the Oases, tastefully designed in mudbrick. The clean, domed rooms have private or shared bathrooms. Owned by local Bedouins, but run by a Swiss woman. Book in advance.

✉ Main street, Farafra
☎ 02-345 8524/012-214 8343; badawya@link.com.eg

Pioneers Hotel (£££)

The first five-star hotel in the Oases, the Pioneers has comfortable air-conditioned rooms and a large swimming pool. Same owners as the equally salmon-pink painted, three-star Mut Talata in Dakhla (☎ 092-821 530).

✉ Kharga ☎ 092-927 982, fax 092-927 983

Shali Lodge (££)

Small mud-brick hotel set in its palm grove, same management as the Adrere Amellal, with peaceful rooms around a small pool.

✉ Sharia Subukha, Siwa ☎ 046-460 1299, fax 046-460 1799

Nile Valley & Lake Nasser

Aswan
Amoun (££–£££)
A great place to relax, this small hotel stands on an island over-looking the Old Cataract and the desert on the other bank of the Nile. Simple but comfortable rooms and a swimming pool.

✉ **Amoun island (free ferry to/from the EgyptAir office)**
☎ **097-313 850, fax 097-317 190**

Sarah's (££)
Larger new hotel, with good size modern rooms that overlook the Nile's First Cataract and the desert on the West Bank. Good value.

✉ **1km south of the Nubia Museum, on the Nile**
☎ **097-327 234**

Sofitel Old Cataract (£££)
This grand hotel, which featured in Agatha Christie's *Death on the Nile*, was opened in 1899 and is probably Egypt's most famous hotel. Filled to the brim with nostalgia, its beautiful rooms command wonderful views over the Nile and Elephantine Island. Tea on the terrace at sunset is a must.

✉ **Sharia Abtal el-Tahrir**
☎ **097-316 000; h1666@accor-hotels.com**

Luxor
Al-Moudira (£££)
Spectacular and luxurious hotel built in local style, on the edge of the desert. The rooms are vast and beautifully decorated with locally made furniture and antiques. The pool is set in the perfumed gardens that overlook the Thebes mountains.

✉ **Daba-iyya, 15km south of the ticket office** ☎ **012-325 1307; moudirahotel@yahoo.com**

Amon el-Gazira (£)
A family-run hotel set amidst fields, with very clean rooms (with and without private bathrooms), a roof terrace with marvellous views of the West Bank and a lovely garden where breakfast is served. Book in advance.

✉ **Geziret el-Bairat, West Bank (near the ferry landing, left at the Mobil petrol station)**
☎ **095-310 912**

Mövenpick Jolie Ville Luxor (£££)
Best family-oriented hotel in Luxor with quiet, if dated, rooms in bungalows in a wonderful well-kept garden. Good food, famous ice-cream, excellent service, great swimming pool and a little zoo for children.

✉ **Crocodile Island, 6km south of Luxor, near the new bridge**
☎ **095-374 855; jolie.ville@ movenpick-lxr.com.eg**

Nur el-Qurna (£)
Beautiful small hotel with large, simply but tastefully decorated rooms with local handmade furniture, celing fans, mosquito nets and view over the sugarcane fields. When full check out the new similar sister hotel Nur al-Balad behind the Medinet Habu temple (☎ 095-426 111)

✉ **Opposite the ticket office, Gurna** ☎ **095-311 430**

Sofitel Old Winter Palace (£££)
Another grand colonial hotel on the Nile with large high-ceilinged rooms and great views, but slow service.

✉ **Sharia Corniche el-Nil, West Bank** ☎ **095-380 422; h1661@accor-hotels.com**

Cruising on Lake Nasser
The easiest way to see the Nubian monuments (▶ 82–3) is to cruise on Lake Nasser. Boats take three or four days to sail from Aswan to Abu Simbel, stopping at temples along the way. Recommended boats include the MS *Eugenie*, with wonderful pre-revolution decor, excellent food, health club and swimming pool, or the smaller *Kasr Ibrim*, owned by the same company Belle Epoque Travel at 17 Sharia Tunis, New Maadi, Cairo ☎ 02-352 8754, fax 02-353 6114.

Suez Zone, Sinai & the Red Sea

Endless Building

Hurghada was a little fishing village until a few years ago but it is now the centre of a solid strip of hotel resorts stretching for many miles north and south along the coast. New resorts are being built further south at Safaga, Quseir and Marsa Alam, forcing serious divers ever further south. The entire Red Sea coast in Egypt, from Suez to the Sudanese border, has been divided up, and apart from some national parks, most has been handed over to developers. So if you are looking for untouched reefs and pristine coastline, come soon.

Suez Zone
Mercure Forsan Island (££)

By far the best and most peaceful hotel in Isma'iliya with comfortable rooms, private beach with watersports and good views over Crocodile Lake.

✉ **Forsan Island, 1.5km southeast of Isma'iliya** ☎ **064-918 040; www.accorhotels.com**

Sonesta (£££)

The better five-star hotel in Port Said, with large comfortable rooms overlooking the canal and town. Swimming pool.

✉ **Sharia Filastin, Port Said** ☎ **066-325 511; www.sonesta.com/egypt_portsaid**

Sinai
Basata (£)

Very popular eco-friendly camp with huts and bungalows on the beach. Those who stay here enjoy the totally relaxed atmosphere. Meals are healthy, natural and communal, there is a desalination plant, and preservation of the coral reefs is high on the agenda.

✉ **Ras el-Burg on the Taba–Nuweiba road, 42km south of Taba** ☎ **069-530 481; www.basata.com**

Four Seasons Sharm el-Shaykh (£££)

Moorish-style super luxurious resort hotel with all facilities, including several pools, watersports and a spa. The rooms are set in lush gardens overlooking the Tiran Straits. The service is friendly and excellent.

✉ **Just north of Naama Bay** ☎ **069-603 555; www.fourseasons.com**

Moon Beach (££)

Holiday resort with simple, comfortable rooms, away from the crowds, with excellent windsurfing facilities.

✉ **At Km98 sign on the road from Ras Sudr to el-Tor, 290km from Sharm el-Sheikh, 190km from Cairo** ☎ **062-401 500, fax 069-401 503; www.gybemasters.co.uk**

Nesima Resort (££)

Beautiful new hotel with lots of domes and arches, simple but comfortable rooms and a great relaxed atmosphere. Has an excellent diving club.

✉ **Mashraba, Dahab** ☎ **069-640 320, fax 069-640 321; nesima@menanet.net**

Pigeon House (£)

One of the cheapest places to stay in Naama Bay with clean modern rooms, across the road from the beach.

✉ **Naama Bay, Sharm el-Sheikh** ☎ **069-600 996, fax 062-600 995**

Sanafir (££)

One of the more characterful hotels in the bay with comfortable Moorish-style rooms set around a pleasant large courtyard and swimming pool. Not on the beach but guests can use the beach of the Aquanaute Diving Club. Large choice of restaurants and the most lively bars in town, including a disco.

✉ **Naama Bay, Sharm el-Sheikh** ☎ **069-600 197, fax 069-600 196; www.sanafirhotel.com**

Seven Heaven (£)

Full range of spotless, newly refurbished accommodation from simple huts to rooms with bathroom and ceiling fan. The complex includes a diving centre, internet café and restaurant. Very friendly service.

✉ **Masbat, Dahab** ☎ **& fax 069-640 080; www.7heaven hotel.com**

La Sirène Resort (££)

Tasteful whitewashed rooms on the beach, with a beach restaurant and diving centre run by Germans.

✉ **Nuweiba, south of the city centre** ☎ **& fax 062-500 701**

Victoria Resort Mövenpick Sharm el-Sheikh (£££)

Huge family resort, popular with European package tourists, with bungalows set in a quiet garden, large swimming pool, and all watersports facilities. Kids' entertainment club.

✉ **Naama Bay, Sharm el-Sheikh** ☎ **062-600 100, fax 062-600 111; www.movenpick-sharm.com**

Red Sea

Dawar el-Omda (££)

Beautiful hotel built in a modern interpretation of traditional Nile-valley architecture, tastefully decorated with antiques and modern furniture designed by young Cairene designers.

✉ **Kafr el-Gouna** ☎ **065-545 060, fax 065-545 561**

El-Giftun Village (££)

One of the oldest holiday resorts with all facilities for windsurfers and divers. Comfortable bungalows are set on the beach. Several bars and restaurants and all watersports are available.

✉ **Resort strip, Hurghada** ☎ **065-442 665, fax 065-442 666**

El-Khan (££)

Smaller hotel with charming rooms set around a peaceful courtyard, overlooking the lagoon. Popular with young Cairenes.

✉ **Kafr el-Gouna** ☎ **065-545 062, fax 065-545 061**

Mangrove Bay Resort (££)

Charming resort, still very quiet, with excellent diving and snorkelling facilities.

✉ **29km south of Quseir** ☎ **02-748 6748, fax 02-760 5458**

Mashrabia Village (££)

Excellent hotel designed in a pseudo-Moorish style with several swimming pools and very good watersports.

✉ **South of the port, Sharia Sheraton, Hurghada** ☎ **065-443 330; www.red-sea.com/sindbad/hotels.html**

Miramar Sheraton (£££)

Architect Michael Graves designed the Miramar on several islands around a lagoon, facing the sea. There is a touch of Disney to the buildings, though the interior design owes much to the Mediterranean. Watersports and a golf course.

✉ **El-Gouna** ☎ **065-545 606, fax 065-545 608**

Mövenpick Sirena Beach (£££)

Peaceful hotel, beautifully designed, with spartan, Nubian-style domed rooms and excellent service. Perfect retreat to get away from it all, with some of Egypt's best snorkelling and diving off the hotel's private beach.

✉ **El-Ouadim Bay, 7km north of Quseir** ☎ **065-332 100, fax 065-332 128**

Red Sea Diving Safari (£–££)

Owner Helmy, a lawyer, environmentalist and enthusiastic diver, has set up a small eco-friendly resort with spotlessly clean and comfortable tents, huts and chalets. Mainly aimed at divers, but non-divers looking for peace and quiet will enjoy this place as well.

✉ **Marsa Shaqara, 20km north of Marsa Alam** ☎ **02-337 1833; www.redsea-divingsafari.com**

Wrecked Ships

There is more to see in the Red Sea than coral gardens and shoals of fish. Several interesting shipwrecks make for good diving expeditions, especially around the dangerous Straits of Gubal, at the mouth of the Gulf of Suez between Hurghada and Sharm el-Sheikh. Diving clubs organise special trips to see these and other wrecks.

Bookshops

Egyptian Music
Cairo is still the centre of Arab culture, so it is a good place to be initiated into the region's music. Kiosks in downtown Cairo sell pirated tapes of inferior quality, so watch what you buy. One of the best places to buy good-quality CDs and tapes of the classics such as Umm Kalthum, Farid el-Atrash and Abdel Wahaab is at Sono Cairo on Sikket Ali Labib Gabr, opposite Radio Cinema, off Sharia Qasr el-Nil, Downtown. For good-quality CDs head for Diwan bookshop (➤ this page), Vibe (✉ Sharia Sayed al-Bakry, Zamalek) or the excellent Mirage Megastore (✉ 71 Sharia Gamiat ed-Dowal el-Arabiya, Mohandeseen).

Cairo
AUC Bookshop
The most extensive range of books on Egypt and the Middle East, many published by the American University Press, as well as the latest English literature.

✉ **American University, 113 Sharia Kasr el-Aini , Hill House on the main Campus, Downtown** ☎ **02-797 5377;**
✉ **16 Sharia Mohammed Thakeb, Zamalek** ☎ **02-339 7045**

Diwan
Excellent, elegant store with books in English and Arabic, a good kids section, DVDs and CDs. Visitors are allowed to browse in the small charming café that serves home-made cakes and drinks. Very good selection.

✉ **159 Sharia 26th of July, Zamalek** ☎ **02-736 2578**

Lehnert and Landrock
Wonderful German, English and French bookshop with a large section on ancient and modern Egypt, Islam and the Arab world. Also copies of interesting old photographs of Cairo and Upper Egypt, new and old postcards and other Egyptian paraphernalia.

✉ **44 Sharia Sherif, Downtown** ☎ **02-393 5324**

Livres de France
Excellent selection of mainly French books on Egypt, well-produced art books and French literature, as well as a few English titles. Good children's section.

✉ **36 Sharia Qasr el-Nil, Downtown** ☎ **02-393 5512**

L'Orientale
Great but expensive bookshop packed full of dusty first editions and more valuable second-hand books and old maps about Egypt, Orientalism or the Middle East in general. You can expect to pay international prices.

✉ **Shop 757, Nile Hilton Shopping Mall, Midan Tahrir, Downtown** ☎ **02-576 2440**

Zamalek Bookstore
A good bookshop with mainly books on Egypt in several European languages, foreign newspapers and magazines and good-quality stationery.

✉ **19 Sharia Shagaret el-Dor, Zamalek** ☎ **02-736 5184**

Alexandria
Al-Mustaqbal
One of the better bookshops in Alexandria, with a good selection of travel books on Egypt and guides in several languages.

✉ **32 Sharia Safiyya Zaghloul**

Luxor
el-Aboudi
Books on Egypt in German, English, French, Spanish and even Japanese, as well as a large selection of postcards and books for children on Egypt, the pharaohs and the pyramids.

✉ **Tourist Bazaar, Corniche el-Nil, next to the Winter Palace Hotel** ☎ **095-373 390**

Gaddis
A great shop with books in many languages covering both modern and ancient Egypt, as well as postcards, Egyptian stationery in papyrus and some good-quality souvenirs.

✉ **Tourist Bazaar, Corniche el-Nil, next to the Winter Palace Hotel** ☎ **095-370 753**

Clothes & Fabrics

Cairo

Atlas Silks

This tiny shop continues a long tradition of making exquisite moiré fabrics in a wide variety of colours as well as tailoring clothes in both Oriental and Western styles. They also make shoes in the same fabric.

✉ el-Badestan alley, Khan el-Khalili ☎ 02-590 6139/591 8833

Haberdashery

Several shops around el-Fishawi café (▶ 93) sell the basic belly dance attire, but the 'king' of belly dance costume shops is Haberdashery, who export to belly dancers all over the world. The showroom is filled with glittering, intricately designed dresses as well as belts, head ornaments, brass cymbals and jewellery. Belly dancers try out the outfits in front of a mirror while performing moves to the loud accompaniment of the latest belly dance tapes.

✉ A dark stairway, signed 'Everything a Belly Dancer Needs', on Sharia Gawhar el-Qayed, Khan el-Khalili near el-Fishawi café

El-Khiyamiya (Tentmakers Bazaar)

Well-preserved roofed market, where the traditional crafts of appliqué work and tentmaking are still practised in several tiny workshops. You can order one of the magnificent tents in a patchwork of Islamic designs, or just a cushion cover or wallhanging for a child's room with folkloric scenes from Egypt.

✉ Just outside Bab Zuwayla, Islamic Cairo

Ouf

A wide range of cheap cotton clothing, funky flowery fabrics, bed sheets, tablecloths and Bedouin-style embroidered dresses is on sale here.

✉ First alley to the left off the Spice Bazaar, which is the alley running along the Madrasa of Sultan Barsbay, off el-Muzz lidin Allah

On Safari

Locally made cotton casual wear, perfect for T-shirts or travelling clothes. The prices are reasonable and the quality good. Watch out for the children's T-shirts with maps of Egypt or a camel caravan.

✉ 10 Sharia Lutfallah, beside the Marriott Hotel, Zamalek ☎ 02-735 1909;
✉ Inside the Nile Hilton, Downtown ☎ 02-579 0845

Tanis

Wonderful cotton and linen fabrics, mostly for furnishings, carrying modern interpretations of original pharaonic motifs or simply camels and palm trees. Look out for the attractive curtain gauze, with Arabic calligraphy or Ottoman star and crescents printed white on white.

✉ World Trade Centre, 1st floor ☎ 02-777 972

Luxor

Winter Akhmim Gallery

Akhmim in Upper Egypt has been known for centuries for its fine handwoven fabrics, and this shop specialises in colourful tablecloths and bedspreads.

✉ Old Winter Palace Hotel, Corniche el-Nil, East Bank ☎ 095-380 422

Shopping Malls

Cairenes, particularly the young, love to hang out in shopping malls. The most popular one is Arcadia (✉ On the Corniche in Bulaq) with mostly imported brands. The First Residence Mall (✉ 35 Sharia Giza, Giza) has the upmarket international designers, while the young flock to the Talaat Harb Complex (✉ Sharia Talaat Harb , Downtown) for casual wear and meeting in bars and fast food outlets.

Aswan *Souk*

Running parallel to the Corniche is Aswan's *souk*, which is more exotic than most in Egypt. It can be very hot during the day, but shops are open late, so take an evening stroll. The market is famous for *karkadeh* (dried hibiscus flowers), from which an infusion is brewed, and for spices and peanuts from Sudan. Brightly coloured Nubian baskets and hand-woven silk scarves are well-made here. Also keep an eye out for magic charms, fetishes and dried crocodiles.

Handicrafts

Art Galleries
Cairo has seen the opening of many art galleries in recent years, many of them Downtown, with a lot more work coming from young Egyptian artists as well as foreigners living in Egypt. Check out *Egypt Today* and *Insight* magazines as well as the daily *Egyptian Gazette* for the latest shows. Places to keep an eye on include Atelier du Caire, 2 Sharia Karim el-Dawla; Mashrabia, 8 Sharia Champollion and the best of all Townhouse Gallery of Contemporary Art, Sharia Hussein Pasha, off Sharia Mahmoud Bassiouni, all Downtown.

Cairo and Environs

Al-Ain Gallery
This gallery exhibits Azza Fahmy's wonderful contemporary silver jewellery, decorated with Arabic inscriptions, as well as stylish traditional metal work, including lanterns and lighting by Randa Fahmy.
✉ **73 Sharia el-Hussayn, Dokki**
☎ **02-349 3940** 🕐 **10AM–9PM**

Al-Khatoun
This stylish shop sells the work of artisans, including cotton fabrics printed with famous belly dancers and movie stars, toys for children, paintings and clothes.
✉ **Behind el-Azhar Mosque, 3 Sharia Mohammed Abduh, Islamic Cairo** ☎ **02-514 7164**

Beit Sherif
When Zaki Sherif returned a few years ago from New York to his native Egypt, he started collecting antiques and royal memorabilia as well as designing his own lighting and furniture. His designs, inspired by the past but with a quirky modern edge to them, can be found in Cairo's trendy bars and restaurants, as well as in hotels in Gouna.
✉ **3A Sharia Bahgat Ali, Zamalek** ☎ **02-736 5689**

Dr Ragab's Papyrus Institute
This institute was founded by former ambassador Dr Hassan Ragab, who revived the making of papyrus to help preserve and promote this ancient Egyptian art. The museum displays the different stages of the making of papyrus and has a sales room on the first floor where you can buy top-quality papyri at top prices.
✉ **Corniche el-Nil close to the Cairo Sheraton, Giza**
☎ **02-748 8177**

Egypt Crafts Center
This is a non-profit-making organisation trying to sell and promote Egyptian crafts, from kilims and embroidered clothes from Northern Sinai to hand-woven tablecloths from Akhmim, recycled paper from Cairo and colourful baskets from Aswan. These high-quality products bear no relation to what is on sale in tatty tourist bazaars. Definitely worth checking out.
✉ **27 Sharia Yahia Ibrahim, 1st floor, apt 8, Zamalek** ☎ **02-736 5123; www.egypts.com**

Hareem Khan
Small jewellery store in the heart of Khan el-Khalili selling old and reproduced Beduin jewellery in silver with brightly coloured semi-precious stones and enamel work.
✉ **6 Sharia al-Haramitiya, Khan el-Khalili** ☎ **02-593 1581**
🕐 **Mon–Sat 9–6**

Khan Misr Tulun
A wonderful treasure trove filled with some of the best handicrafts from all over Egypt. A world away from most of what is on sale in Khan el-Khalili.
✉ **Facing the main entrance of the Ibn Tulun Mosque, Sayyida Zaynab** ☎ **02-365 2227**
🕐 **10AM–5PM. Closed Sat, Sun**

Makan
Interesting contemporary design based on the traditional ancient Egyptian and Islamic motifs, all by local designers and artists.
✉ **4 Sharia Ismail Mohammed, Zamalek** ☎ **02-738 2632**

Nagada

Beautiful hand-woven cotton fabrics and tablecloths in natural colours, fabric lanterns and fabulous pottery made in the village of Tunis in el-Faiyum, all tastefully displayed in this flat.

✉ **8 Sharia Dar El-Shefa, 3rd floor, Garden City** ☎ **02 792 3249** 🕐 **Mon–Sat 10–2, afternoons by appointment**

Nomad Gallery

A floor of an elegant Zamalek residence filled with original Bedouin jewellery and rugs, as well as traditional designs in silver, and textiles and many types of baskets, mostly hand-made in Egypt.

✉ **14 Saraya el-Gezira, 1st floor, Zamalek (and smaller branch in garden of the Cairo Marriott Hotel, Zamalek)** ☎ **02-736 1917**

Ramses Wissa Wassef

This arts centre has been weaving carpets since 1952 and its work has been admired and collected by museums and galleries around the world. The carpets are woven by villagers under the eye of different generations of the Wissa Wassef family.

✉ **Off the Saqqara Road, 4km south of Giza, Harraniya** ☎ **02-285 0403** 🕐 **Daily 10–5**

Senouhi

Worth looking for, this hard-to-find shop (ring the doorbell if the door is closed) is an Aladdin's cave filled with Wissa Wasef carpets, old jewellery, embroidered clothes from Siwa, old postcards and books and felt puppets for children. Look out for the embroidered trousers and waistcoats for

both adults and children, and the 1950s-style postcards.

✉ **54 Shari Abdel Khaleq Sarwat, 5th floor, apt 51, near Midan Opera** ☎ **02-391 0955**

Sheba Gallery

An interesting gallery with a selection of traditional and contemporary silver jewellery, textiles, pottery and small gifts.

✉ **6 Sharia Sri Lanka, Zamalek** ☎ **02-735 9192**

El-Faiyum

Pottery School of Michel and Evelyne Pastore

This Swiss couple of potters started a pottery school for local children in this artists' village. You can see them at work or buy their fabulous pottery from the shop. Highly recommended and worth the detour. (Shop in Cairo, ▶ Nagada 108)

✉ **Village of Tunis, on the road to Wadi Rayyan, along Qarun Lake** ☎ **02-792 3249**

Luxor

Fair Trade Center Luxor Outlet

This lovely shop sells handicrafts from non-governmental organisation projects all over Egypt, and particularly from the nearby villages of Hegaza and Garagos. Very good selection and prices.

✉ **Sharia el-Karnak** ☎ **095-387 015**

Sharm el-Sheikh

Aladin

Tiny shop with small antiques, Bedouin textiles and a good selection of glass beads, scarabs and hand-carved sea urchin bones.

✉ **In the El-Diar Hotel, Naama Bay** ☎ **062-600 826**

Glass Blowing

Glass making was probably introduced in Egypt by Asian artisans during the reign of Tuthmosis III, around 1500 BC, and happily it is still being practised. The rustic Muski glass is still produced by blowing recycled glass into new shapes: green and brown glass comes from beer and wine bottles; for clear glass manganese is added to the mixture, while copper filings are added to make turquoise glass. The most famous glass maker is el-Daour in Cairo, which can be reached by foot from Bab el-Futuh (▶ 34). Stand outside the gate and walk across the small square, turn right up Sharia el-Hussariya. Take the first left onto Sharia El-Beiraqdar and follow the narrow twisting alley to the end, which runs into the factory (open Sun–Thu 7:30AM–sunset).

Bedouins

Sinai's dwindling community of Bedouins are increasingly being settled into dull concrete villages without any employment prospects, and only a few remain semi-nomadic. The coastline is being developed, with most profits going to Cairene entrepreneurs and foreign companies, not to the local community. The largest Bedouin settlement is in el-Arish in Northern Sinai, which has a Bedouin market on Thursdays.

Children's Attractions

Children's Lunch

Don't worry about taking children to restaurants. Egyptians adore children, especially little ones, and you will usually find one or more waiters cooing over your child or offering to entertain them. Children will particularly like some of the more unusual restaurants such as Felfela Garden (➤ 92–93) in Downtown Cairo, with its displays of live animals, and Andrea in Giza (➤ 92) which offers a playground, occasional donkey rides and the possibility of watching bread being baked.

Arts

Cairo Puppet Theatre

Great puppet theatre in Arabic, but the show is exciting enough even if you don't understand.

✉ Ezbekiya Gardens, Downtown ☎ 02-591 0954 ⏲ Oct–Apr, Thu–Sun

Fagnoon Art School

Artist Mohammed Allam runs this great art school near Saqqara, where kids can let their imagination run wild and work with materials such as wrought iron, clay, paint, woodwork etc.

✉ Saqqara Road, Sabil Om Hashim ☎ 012-214 7136 /02 815 1014

Felucca Sailing

One of the most relaxing things to do on a hot afternoon is to hire a felucca (➤ 78), take a picnic and watch life along the river and its banks. The best place to do it is Aswan, but it is fun everywhere, even in Cairo. Boatmen usually let children steer for a while.

Glass-bottomed Boats

Most resorts, both in Sinai and along the Red Sea, offer daily trips in glass-bottomed boats, which allow visitors who are not so keen on diving or snorkelling the chance to explore the wonders of the Red Sea.

Horse Riding

Children will love riding through the desert near the pyramids. Rather than getting hassled by persistent horse- and camel-drivers around the pyramids, use the recommended stables

Arabian Horse Stable

The stable provides camels, donkeys and horses for both adults and children to explore the countryside or the desert on the West Bank, Luxor.

✉ Behind the Mobil petrol station, near the ferry landing on the West Bank, Luxor ☎ 095-310 024 ⏲ Daily

International Equestrian Club

The best stables around with excellent horses and friendly staff. Very good riding lessons for kids, but book in advance.

✉ On Saqqara Road at the end of al-Muneeb ring road ☎ 02-742 7654 ⏲ Daily

Museums

el-Mathaf el-Masri (Egyptian Museum)

This vast museum is wonderful for both children and adults alike. Children will be particularly fascinated by Tutankhamun's treasure (including bows, daggers and chariots), the mummy room and models representing ancient Egyptian life on the first floor (➤ 23).

✉ Midan Tahrir, Cairo ☎ 02-575 4319 ⏲ Sat–Thu 9–4:45, Fri 9–11:15, 1:30–4 ⓦ Moderate; mummies expensive

Mathaf el-Atfaal (Children's Museum)

Fascinating museum with interactive displays of Pharaonic Egypt, children's dress through the ages, and various halls about the desert and the Nile.

✉ Forest Park, Heliopolis ☎ 02-639 9915 ⏲ Daily 9–4 ⓦ Moderate

Mathaf el-Mumia (Mummification Museum)

This modern museum explains the process of mummification, which played such an important role in ancient Egyptian funerary rituals. Mummies of both animals and humans are well displayed, as well as the instruments used (▶ 68).

✉ On the East Bank Corniche, Luxor 🕙 9–1, 4–9 in winter, 5–10PM in summer 💷 Moderate

Mathaf el-Zira'a (Agricultural Museum)

The oldest agricultural museum in the world contains a large collection of stuffed animals and lively, life-size reproductions of Egyptian village life. The large garden has a huge variety of trees.

✉ Next to 6 October Bridge Sharia Wizaret al-Ziraa, Doqqi 🕾 02-702 933 🕙 Tue–Sun 9–1.30. Closed Mon 💷 Cheap

Theme Parks

Cairo Land

A large theme park with fairground-type rides, including a water ride. Cairo Land's Acropolis theatre, a disco by night, hosts an afternoon puppet show with singing and dancing aimed at younger children.

✉ 1 Sharia Salah Salem, Cairo 🕾 02-364 0430 🕙 Daily 💷 Expensive

Crazy Water

A fun theme park with a variety of water slides, a wave pool, a children's pool and a playground area with sand, slides and tunnels.

✉ Next to 6th of October City, Alexandria-Cairo Desert Road

🕾 02-781 4564 🕙 Daily 10–10 💷 Expensive

Dr Ragab's Pharaonic Village

A 2-hour guided tour by boat, quite kitsch but fun, through the Canal of Mythology, taking in scenes of ancient Egyptian rural life, and ending at a temple with a sacred lake. Possibility of dressing like a pharaoh and posing for a picture. There is also a restaurant, café and small playground.

✉ Jacob's Island, Sakiet Miky, Giza, Cairo 🕾 02-571 8675; www.touregypt.net/village 🕙 Daily 9–5 (winter), 9–9 (summer) 💷 Expensive

Zoos & Gardens

Al-Fustat Garden

Very busy during weekends and holidays, this is a favourite picnic spot for Cairene families, with large playgrounds.

✉ Sharia Salah Salem, next to Cairo Lane 🕾 02-363 9229

Cairo Zoological Gardens

Built in 1891, this was once one of the world's greatest zoos, but today it is struggling to survive. Kids are allowed to feed the animals so they love it.

✉ Midan el-Gamaa, Giza 🕾 02-570 8895 🕙 Daily 9–4 💷 Cheap

Gineenat el-Samak (Fish Garden)

About 200 displays of tropical fish set into several grottoes and a labyrinth of little alleys which are great fun for children to explore.

✉ Gabalaya Park, Sharia Umm Kulthum, Zamalek 🕙 Daily 8:30–3 💷 Cheap

Baby Gear

In most tourist centres it is no problem finding the baby essentials. Pharmacies and better grocery shops sell powdered milk and jars of puréed food. Be warned that nappies made in Egypt are not as efficient as those sold in Europe, and even though imported varieties are readily available it may be useful to take enough with you for night use. Sunblock for children is often but not always available, and most necessary at all times. Bring your own armbands and inflatable rings for the sea and pools, as well as rubber shoes to protect against corals in the Red Sea.

Nightclubs & Discos

Disco Etiquette

Some nightclubs in five-star hotels will accept only members and hotel residents on busy evenings. Elsewhere, single men may be refused in favour of couples or mixed groups. Some places will refuse entry to single women, while others will let them in for free. Egyptians usually dress up to go out, so leave the shorts at home, even on hot nights. Thursday and Friday nights are the busiest nights.

The best belly dancers perform at the nightclubs of five-star hotels. There is usually an early performance with dinner at 8–9PM, but most Egyptians and Arabs wait for the late show, which can happen anytime between 1 and 3AM. For a rougher, more popular belly dance show head for one of the Downtown nightclubs around Ezbekiya: there, as it gets later and more money gets thrown at the girls, so the best dancers take to the floor. Do not be offended if you are seated at the back of the hall, as foreigners are not expected to know the art of throwing money on stage.

Cairo

Africana

African disco with a cool atmosphere, good music (African and Egyptian) and lively dancing. An easier more relaxed environment for women who like to dance on their own.
✉ Sharia el-Ahram, Giza
🕐 9PM–3AM

Bam-Bu

Great disco and lounge bar with excellent DJs, set in Asian decor and with views on the Nile. It's expensive but worth going to once but it gets very busy on a Thursday and Friday night.
✉ Casino El-Shagara, Corniche el-Nil, Bulaq, opposite the World Trade Centre
☎ 02-579 6512 🕐 9PM–3AM

Cairo Jazz Club

Although in an unlikely place, the Cairo Jazz Club hosts regular live jazz sessions from foreign and Egyptian musicians. There's always a great atmosphere. Serves good *mezze* and salads, too.
✉ 197, 26th of July Street, beside the Zamalek Bridge, Aguza ☎ 02-354 9939; www.cairojazzclub.com
🕐 7PM–early morning

Latex

Upmarket disco with good foreign and local DJs, popular with Cairo's young, trendy and rich crowd.
✉ Nile Hilton Hotel, Corniche el-Nil, Downtown ☎ 02-578 0666 🕐 10PM–4AM

El-Morocco

This bar-restaurant turns into a lively disco later at night, very popular with young wealthy Cairenes who dance to Western and Egyptian music. Outside seating area if you want to escape the crowds.
✉ Blue Nile boat, 9 Saray El-Gezira, Zamalek
☎ 02-735 3114

Palmyra

In an authentic 1950s hall, the *madame* with monocle will lead you to your seats and encourage you to drink alcohol while always keeping an eye out that the Gulf Arabs do not overdo it with the plump belly dancers. Recommended if you want something a little bit different.
✉ Alley off 26th July Street, Ezbekiya 🕐 10PM–4AM

Sharm el-Shaykh Pacha

The famous Ibizian Club has just opened its first club in the Middle East and Africa, in Sharm, and it is bound to be the venue to be seen at for a while.
✉ Sanafir Hotel, Naama Bay
☎ 069-600 197 🕐 10PM–4AM

Cinema & Theatre

Cinema
Film and theatre listings appear in the daily *Egyptian Gazette*, the *Egyptian Mail on Sunday*, the weekly *al-Ahram* and the monthly *Insight* and *Egypt Today* magazines. Arabic films are rarely subtitled but quite a few cinemas (main ones listed below) offer English films with or without Arabic subtitles.

Cairo
Metro
✉ 35 Sharia Talaat Harb, Downtown ☎ 02-393 7566

MGM
✉ 4th floor Maadi Grand Mall ☎ 02-519 5388

New Odeon
✉ Cairo Sheraton, Sharia el-Galaa, Giza ☎ 02-760 6081

Ramses Hilton I & II
✉ 7th floor of hotel's annex shopping mall, Corniche el-Nil ☎ 02-574 7436

Renaissance
Cairo's swishest.
✉ World Trade Centre, 1191 Corniche el-Nil, Boulaq ☎ 02-578 4915

Theatre

Cairo
Al-Sawy Cultural Center
Very active centre with performances every night of experimental theatre, Arabic or jazz concerts, lectures and screenings of films and documentaries.
✉ Sharia 26th of July, Zamalek, under the bridge to Agouza ☎ 02-736 6178

Beit el-Harrawi
Various performances of Arabic music and theatre particulary during the Ramadan nights. On the first Thursday of every month there is a free classical Arab music concert.
✉ Behind el-Azhar Mosque, Islamic Cairo ☎ 02-735 7001

Cairo Opera House
The main hall of the opera house has 1,200 seats to accomodate the audiences of Egyptian and prestigious international ballet, opera and theatre performances. The smaller hall can hold 500. There is also an open-air theatre. Advance booking is recommended. Men should wear jacket and tie for all performances (except for some in the open-air theatre).
✉ Gezira Exhibition Grounds, Gezira ☎ 02-737 0603

Falaki Theatre
Excellent theatre for Western-style performances and regular concerts.
✉ American University in Cairo, Sharia Falaki, Downtown
☎ 02-794 2964
🕐 Oct–May

Alexandria
Alexandria Centre of Arts
Great cultural centre in a white-washed villa, with contemporary art exhibitions, free concerts, library and cinema.
✉ 1 Tariq el-Hurreya
☎ 03-495 6633

Sayed Darwish Theatre
Beautifully restored opera house hosting regular performances of opera, theatre and ballet.
✉ 22 Tariq el-Hurreya, opposite Cinema Royale
☎ 03-486 5602

Whirling Dervishes
The Mawlawiyya are the Egyptian branch of the Sufi sect founded in the 13th century in Konya (Turkey), known as the Whirling Dervishes. A good tourist show of these Whirling Dervishes is staged by the Tannoura Egyptian Heritage Dance Troupe at the Sarayat al-Gabal Theatre, Citadel, Sharia Salah Salem (▶ 41). Performances take place every Saturday, Monday and Wednesday at 8:30PM, tickets are free.

Sports

Cairo Hash House Harriers

The Hash House Harriers meet every Friday, two hours before sunset, to jog, walk or run at different locations near Cairo. For information check website www.cairohash.com or www.instantweb.com/h/ cairohash. The Delta Hash House Harriers organise runs and walks around Alexandria for everyone, every Friday at 2PM from September to June, starting from the Centro de Portugal, Sharia Kafr Abduh in Roushdi. Call ☎ 03-582 4309 for details.

Cycling

The Cairo Cyclists meet each Friday and Saturday at 7AM at the front gate of the Cairo American College, 1 Midan Digla, Maadi for a day's cycling.
☎ 352 6310

Desert Driving

Heading off into remote areas of the desert is becoming increasingly popular, but still takes serious planning, reliable equipment and an experienced guide. Some of the best tour guides are:

Abdallah Baghi

Abdallah organises great trips in the Great Sand Sea or elsewhere in and around Siwa for the day or several days, and can arrange all the permits needed. All trips are done by 4WD and Abdallah is a very knowledgeable guide, passionate about the oasis and the desert.
☎ 010-166 4294;
shali55@hotmail.com

Al-Badawiya

Arrange highly recommended treks throughout the Western Desert and other areas of Egypt.
☎ 02-575 8076;
www.badawiya.com

Amr Shannon

An artist, who has been leading small groups through Egypt's deserts for more than 20 years.
☎ 02-519 6894;
ashannon@internetegypt.com

Peter Gaballa

Peter leads great safaris through the desert either with chauffeured jeeps or self-drive if you are up to it. He also teaches driving courses and survival techniques in the desert. the most fabulous trips are the 14-days in the Great Sand Sea or to Uweynat.
☎ 012-314 2388;
www.egyptoffroad.com

Fishing

Fishing is forbidden off the Sinai shores, but allowed elsewhere in the Red Sea, on the Mediterranean and on the Nile. Boats and guides can be rented in Alexandria and Hurghada. More information is available from The Shooting Club in Cairo
☎ 02-337 3337;
www.shootingclubegypt.com

African Angler in Aswan

Big game fresh water fishing safaris are operated on Lake Nasser, a great place to find the massive Nile perch, the Tiger fish and Vundu catfish.
☎ 097-309 748/012-749 1892;
www.african-angler.co.uk

Wild Nuba

This company offers well-run fishing safaris.
☎ 097-309 191;
www.lakenasseradventure.com

Golf

Equipment can be rented but golf has become a fashionable sport and courses are very busy.

Katameya Heights Golf & Tennis Resort

27 holes of championship golf, practice facilities and a golf academy, set amid endless rolling hills.
✉ New Cairo City (Fifth District), Ring Road, West Heliopolis ☎ 02-758 0512; www.katameya.com

Mena House Golf Course

The oldest and most mature golf course in Egypt; 18

holes (played on 9 fairways).
✉ Mena House Oberoi, Sharia el-Haram, Giza ☎ 02-383 3222;
www.oberoihotels.com/mena.htm

Horse-racing

Horse-racing takes place on Saturdays and Sundays from October to May, starting at 1PM, at the Hippodrome Course (✉ Heliopolis in Cairo ☎ 02-241 7086), or at the Smouha Race Course in Alexandria. Horse-races also take place on weekends at the Gezira Club (✉ Saraya el-Gezira ☎ 02-736 0434).

Horse Riding

It makes for a fun day out to go by horse from Giza to Saqqara, riding between the villages and the desert. The best stables are the International Equestrian Club (☎ 02-742 7654), on Saqqara Rd at the end of al-Muneeb ring road, who have very good horses and provide excellent riding lessons for kids and adults (book in advance). The Saqqara Country Club (✉ Saqqara Rd to Abu el Nomros ☎ 02-384 6115, fax 02-385 0577) has good stables and riding facilities (temporary memberships are available).

Luxor
The Arabian Horse Stable
Has both horses and camels available by the hour for exploring the antiquities or to ride along the Nile.
✉ Behind the Mobil Oil petrol station on the West Bank
☎ 095-310 024

Sharm el-Sheikh
The Fayrouz Hilton
Organises horse trips into the Sinai desert.
☎ 062-600 136, fax 062-601 040

Scuba Diving
All diving centres offer equipment rental and organise boat excursions and diving courses. The main Red Sea resorts (► 89) all have shops where you can buy your own snorkelling and diving equipment. The Cairo Divers Club (☎ 02-570 3242) meets the first Monday of every month at the Semiramis InterContinental in Garden City.

Diving Centres

Dahab
Nesima Diving Centre
✉ Nesima Hotel
☎ 069-640 320;
www.nesima.com

Orca Dive Club
☎ 069-640 020;
orcadive_eg@yahoo.com

Hurghada
Aquanaut Red Sea
☎ 065-549 891;
www.acquanaut.net

Red Sea Safari
☎ 02-337 1833; www.redsea-divingsafari.com

Easy Diver
✉ Three Corners Village
☎ 065-548 816;
www.easydivers-redsea.com

Nuweiba
Emperor Divers
✉ At Nuweiba Hilton
☎ 069-520 321;
www.emperordivers.com

Quseir
Sub Ex Dive Centre
✉ Movenpick
☎ 065-332 100

Sharm el-Sheikh
Sinai Divers
☎ 069-600 150;
www.sinaidivers.com

Oonas Diving Centre
☎ 069-600 581;
www.oonasdivers.com

Red Sea Diving College
✉ Naama Bay ☎ 069-600 313;
www.redseacollege.com

Soccer Crazy
Egyptians are mad about football and when Egypt or one of the local teams plays the streets are empty and silent. From September to May there are football matches every Friday at 3PM and Sunday afternoon. Cairo has two popular teams, Ahli and Zamalek, and taxi drivers often judge your character upon which team you support.

What's On When

Ramadan
During the month of Ramadan, most Muslim Egyptians abstain from drinking, eating, smoking and other pleasures from sunrise to sunset. Businesses work more or less part time and the traffic becomes absolutely frantic in the hour before sunset, as everyone tries to get home to break the fast. In the evening families go to the area around el-Husayn Mosque in Cairo for amusement, tea and a waterpipe. Bars, if open at all, don't serve alcohol to Egyptians, not even to Copts, and it is advisable to take your passport for this reason.

For Egyptian festivals information:
www.festival.cpmeg

Egypt's world wide web address is at:
http://pharos.bu.edu/Egypt /Home.html

Islamic Festivals
The Islamic calendar is based on a lunar cycle of 12 months of 29 or 30 days, so the Muslim year is 11 days shorter than the Western or Gregorian calendar. This makes it difficult to give exact dates for Muslim festivals. To be sure, check with the Egyptian Tourist Authority.
Ras al-Sana (Islamic New Year): first of the month of Muharram
Aid el-Fitr: end of Ramadan
Aid el-Adha (Bayram): holiday when sheep are slaughtered to commemorate Abraham's sacrifice

Moulids
Moulids or celebrations of saints' days take place throughout the year and throughout Egypt. The Moulid el-Nabi (Birthday of the Prophet) is celebrated all over the country, especially near the el-Husayn Mosque (➤ 43) in Cairo. The most important *moulids* such as el-Husayn and Sayyida Zeinab in Cairo, Sayyid el-Badawi in Tanta and Abu el-Haggag in Luxor attract thousands and sometimes millions of believers from all over Egypt and the Islamic world. There are also a few Coptic *moulids* and one Jewish *moulid*.

January
• 7th Jan: Coptic Christmas after 43 days of abstaining from animal products
• End of Jan–beginning Feb: Cairo International Book Fair

February
• International Fishing Competition that takes place in Hurghada ☎ 02-395 3953

• 22 Feb: Dawn rays of the sun reach the sanctuary at Abu Simbel temple
• Luxor Marathon, popular annual event

March/April
• Coptic Easter, date varies up to five weeks after Western Easter
• Sham el-Nessim: public holiday the Monday after Coptic Easter, dating from pharaonic times, celebrating the onset of spring

August
• Folkloric Art Festival takes place in Ismailiya
☎ 02-354 7818

September
• International Festival for Experimental Theatre in Cairo
• Alexandria International Film Festival ☎ 03-574 112

October
• After the cotton harvest, *moulid* of Sayyid el-Badawi in Tanta
• Pharaoh's Rally (Siag Travel ☎ 02-385 6022)
• 22 Oct: Dawn rays of the sun reach the sanctuary at Abu Simbel temple

November
• International Fishing Competition in Sharm el-Sheikh ☎ 02-395 3953
• 4th Nov: Luxor Festival (dance and music)

December
• Cairo International Film Festival ☎ 02-516 1422
• International Nile Regatta Festival in Cairo and Luxor ☎ 02-393 4350

Practical
Matters

Before You Go   118
When You Are There   119–23
Language   124

الهيئة العامة
للتجميل والنظافة

**WELCOME IN
CAIRO**

Above: *many medicines are
available without prescription*
Right: *welcoming sign in
Cairo's Ramses Square*

117

TIME DIFFERENCES

GMT	Egypt	Germany	USA (NY)	Netherlands	Spain
→ 12 noon	→ 2PM	→ 1PM	← 7AM	→ 1PM	→ 1PM

BEFORE YOU GO

WHAT YOU NEED

● Required ○ Suggested ▲ Not required	Some countries require a passport to remain valid for a minimum period (usually at least six months) beyond the date of entry – contact their consulate or embassy or your travel agent for details.	UK	Germany	USA	Netherlands	Spain
Passport		●	●	●	●	●
Visa (regulations can change – check before booking your journey)		●	●	●	●	●
Onward or Return Ticket		▲	▲	▲	▲	▲
Health Inoculations (polio, tetanus, hepatitis)		○	○	○	○	○
Health Documentation (► 123, Health)		▲	▲	▲	▲	▲
Travel Insurance		○	○	○	○	○
Driving Licence (International)		●	●	●	●	●
Car Insurance Certificate (if own car)		●	●	●	●	●
Car Registration Document (if own car)		●	●	●	●	●

WHEN TO GO

Cairo

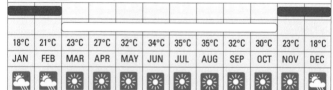

High season

Low season

18°C	21°C	23°C	27°C	32°C	34°C	35°C	35°C	32°C	30°C	23°C	18°C
JAN	FEB	MAR	APR	MAY	JUN	JUL	AUG	SEP	OCT	NOV	DEC

 Sun   Sunshine/Showers

TOURIST OFFICES

In the UK
Egyptian State Tourist Office
Egyptian House
170 Piccadilly
London W1V 9DD
☎ 020-7493 5283
egypt@freenetname.co.uk

In the USA
Egyptian Tourist Authority
8383 Wilshire Boulevard
Suite 215, Beverly Hills,
Los Angeles
CA90211
☎ 213-781 7676
Fax 213-653 8961

630 Fifth Avenue
Suite 1706
New York NY10111
☎ 0212-332 2570
Fax 0212-956 6439
www.interoz.com/egypt

POLICE 122

TOURIST POLICE 126

FIRE 180

AMBULANCE 123

ANGLO-AMERICAN HOSPITAL IN CAIRO 02-735 6162

WHEN YOU ARE THERE

ARRIVING

The national airline, EgyptAir, operates flights from most European capitals and the US to Cairo, and a few to Luxor. Charter holidays are available to Luxor, Hurghada and Sinai. The easiest way into town is by limousine (pre-paid in the arrivals hall, fixed prices).

Cairo International Airport **Journey times**
Distance to city centre

25 kilometres

🚊	N/A
🚌	45 minutes
🚗	35–45 minutes

Luxor International Airport **Journey times**
Distance to city centre

7 kilometres

🚊	N/A
🚌	N/A
🚗	15 minutes

MONEY

The Egyptian pound (LE, *guineh* in Arabic) is divided into 100 piastres (PT, *irsh* in Arabic). There are notes for 5, 10, 25 and 50 piastres and 1, 5, 10, 20, 50, and 100 pounds, and coins for 5, 10 and 25 piastres. Travellers' cheques, preferably in US$, can be changed in banks and exchange bureaux (transaction charge). Credit cards are widely accepted at banks, hotels and up-market restaurants, but it is wise to check first. Many five-star hotels and banks in tourist resorts have automatic cash dispensing machines.

TIME

🕐 Egypt stays two hours ahead of GMT most of the year, except during summer time (beginning of May to beginning of October), when it is three hours ahead. Time is a looser concept in Egypt than in Europe: five minutes can mean a few hours, and tomorrow can easily mean next week.

CUSTOMS

→ **YES**

Declare video cameras and computers on a D-form on arrival, and show on departure. In case of theft report to the police or pay 100 per cent duty.
Alcohol: 1l of liquor or wine
Cigarettes: 200 *or*
Cigars: 50 *or*
Tobacco: 250g
Perfume: 1l *or*
Toilet water: 1l

In Luxor and Cairo airports there are duty free shops where you can buy another four litres of alcohol on arrival.

— **NO**

Drugs, firearms. It is forbidden to export genuine Egyptian antiques from Egypt.

119

UK	Germany	Netherlands	Spain	US
02-794 0850	02-736 0015	02-735 1936	02-735 6437	02-795 7371

WHEN YOU ARE THERE

TOURIST OFFICES

Alexandria
- Ramleh Station
  Sharia Saad Zaghloul
  ☎ 03-480 7611
- Misr Railway Station
  ☎ 03-492 5985

Aswan
- Midal el-Mahatta, next to
  the train station
  ☎ 097-312 811

Cairo
- 5 Sharia Adly, Downtown
  ☎ 02-391 3454
- Giza Pyramids
  ☎ 02-385 0259
- Ramses Railway Station
  ☎ 02-579 0767

El Faiyum
- Midan Qarun
  ☎ 084-347 298

Hurghada
- Resort Strip
  ☎ 065-444 420

Luxor
- Corniche el-Nil
  ☎ 095-372 215
- Luxor Airport
  ☎ 095-373 2215

Port Said
- Sharia Filastin 8
  ☎ 066-235 289

NATIONAL HOLIDAYS

J	F	M	A	M	J	J	A	S	O	N	D
1			2	1		1			2		1

1 Jan	New Year's Day
7 Jan	Coptic Christmas Day
April	Coptic Easter Sunday (day before Sham el-Nessim)
April	Sham el-Nessim
25 Apr	Liberation Day
1 May	Labour Day
23 Jul	Revolution Day
6 Oct	Armed Forces Day

The Islamic New Year, Prophet's Birthday, Aid el-Fitr
(3 days) and Aid el-Adha (4 days) are also national
holidays (dates vary). In addition Egypt observes the
traditional feast days of the Muslim Year and the
month of fasting, Ramadan (► 116). The dates of
these follow the lunar calendar and therefore move
backwards by 11 days a year.

OPENING HOURS

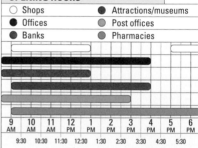

○ Shops	● Attractions/museums
● Offices	○ Post offices
● Banks	● Pharmacies

Times given may vary. In tourist areas shops tend to
stay open all day until late at night, especially in high
season. In Ramadan everything tends to open an hour
later and close an hour or two earlier, but shops and
some offices reopen 8–10PM. Banks in tourist areas
often stay open all day, until late at night. Banks at
Cairo Airport and Marriott and Nile Hilton hotels in
Cairo are open 24 hours. Museums and monuments
close on Friday for prayers 11–1 (12–2, summer). Post
Offices are open from Saturday until Thursday.
Pharmacies are often open until 9PM or later.

DRIVE ON THE RIGHT

TOILETS BASIC

Use hotels and restaurants

PUBLIC TRANSPORT

 Internal Flights EgyptAir flies daily from Cairo to most of Egypt's main cities, and Air Sinai flies from Cairo to Hurghada, Sinai and Tel Aviv. Both can be booked through EgyptAir offices (☎ 02-579 3048). The private airline Orascom (☎ 065-547 934) flies from Cairo and Luxor to el-Gouna.

 Trains The Egyptian State Railway services the Nile Valley, Alexandria, Suez, Port Said and Mersa Matruh. Buy tickets in advance. Wagon-Lits (☎ 02-576 1319) operate a sleeper train from Cairo to Luxor and Aswan, and fast trains to Alexandria. Book in advance from Ramses Station in Cairo (☎ 02-574 9474; www.sleepingtrains.com).

Buses Buses run from Cairo to most cities in Egypt. Tickets for air-conditioned buses should be booked in advance. Buses now leave from the Turgoman Garage (Sharia al-Gisr, Bulaq, 1km north of Ramses station). All the different companies have their ticket cabin at this garage, so it might take a little search before you get to the right one. Superjet and Golden Rocket operate fast buses to Alexandria and Marsa Matruh. Buses for Sinai still stop at the old Sinai terminal on Sharia Ramses in Abbasiya as well, while buses for El-Faiyum leave from under the Munib Bridge in Giza.

 Urban Transport Cairo's buses are usually packed to the roof and women are often hassled, so it is advisable to use taxis (► below), which are cheap and more comfortable. The metro is clean and easy to use, especially from Downtown Cairo to Coptic Cairo or Heliopolis.

CAR RENTAL

 Rent a car with a driver. After recent terrorist attacks it is almost impossible to drive anywhere in Egypt without the protection of an armed convoy. You could be asked for your papers at road-blocks and may have to turn back.

TAXIS

 Collective service taxis are usually faster than buses and charge similar rates to bus fares. They usually operate from near bus stations and leave as soon as they have six or seven passengers on board.

DRIVING

 Speed limits on all highways: **100kph**

 Speed limits on main roads: **90kph**

 Speed limits in urban centres: **50kph**

Avoid driving in the dark outside the city as some drivers do not use their lights or switch them on at the last minute, blinding you. Just after sunset people walk their animals home and there is general chaos on rural roads.

 Seatbelts are now compulsory.

 There are many petrol (benzene) stations in the main towns, but fewer out in the countryside. Petrol stations are serviced, not self-serve. Always fill your tank to the limit, and clean the oil filter regularly, as dust and impurities in the petrol tend to clog up the engine. Larger petrol stations are often open until late at night. Petrol is cheaper than in Europe and the US.

 Egyptian car mechanics are often masters of invention and can usually be relied upon to fix a broken down car. There are also usually people at hand to help you push your car to the next garage or to the side of the road. Most garages stock a good range of spare parts.

121

PERSONAL SAFETY

Petty crime remains rare in Egypt but like everywhere else you should watch your belongings in busy tourist areas and on full buses.

- Leave money and valuables in the hotel safe. Carry only what you need.
- There is a crackdown on drugs, with fines for possession, and life imprisonment or hanging for anyone convicted of dealing or smuggling.
- Foreigners travelling between cities sometimes have to move in a police-protected convoy. There are roadblocks in the main cities at night.

Tourist Police assistance:
☎ 126

Safety in Middle Egypt
The area around Asyut, Dairut and Mallawi has long been a stronghold for Islamic fundamentalists. Since the early 1990s they have targetted foreigners in an attempt to destabilise the country, which depends on tourism. Their campaign of attacks against trains, cruise boats and tourist buses culminated in the attack in 1997 at Deir el-Bahari in Luxor, in which 58 foreigners and 10 Egyptians were killed. In spite of a significant tightening of security, at the time of writing it is still advisable to avoid this area.

ELECTRICITY

The power supply in Egypt is 220 volts. Sockets take two-round-pin plugs. British visitors will need an adaptor, US visitors a voltage transformer.

TELEPHONES

Local calls can be made from coin-operated phone boxes, hotels and kiosks. International calls can be made from Telephone and Telegraph (TT) offices. The main branches, at Midan el-Tahrir and at 8 Sharia Adly, are open 24 hours, while other branches are open 7AM–10PM daily. Look for the orange direct-dial telephones which take phone cards that are on sale there. Otherwise, go through an operator, who will charge you a minimum 3 minutes for opening the line. Calls are cheapest between 8PM and 8AM.

International Dialling Codes

From Egypt to:	
UK:	00 44
Germany:	00 49
USA:	00 1
Netherlands:	00 31
Spain:	00 34

POST

Stamps can bought at post offices, souvenir shops and hotel newsagents. Airmail letters take about a week to arrive in Europe, a little longer for the USA and Australia. Post your letters in your hotel or use a post office; avoid street letterboxes. Cairo's main post office (open 24 hours) is on Midan el-Ataba.

TIPS/GRATUITIES

Yes ✓ No ✗		
Restaurants (service not included)	✓	8–10%
Restaurants (service included)	✓	change
Cafés/bars	✓	10%
Taxis (negotiate the price first)	✓	5–10%
Museum and site guides	✓	LE5–10
Chambermaids	✓	LE10–15
Porters	✓	LE10–20
Car Parking	✓	PT50
Toilets	✓	PT25–50

PHOTOGRAPHY

What to photograph: everything (exceptions below) – the light in Egypt is wonderful.

What not to photograph: bridges, airports, railway stations, government buildings, dams or anything the authorities consider important to their security. Ask permission before photographing people. Most museums sell special tickets for the use of cameras and videos.

Buying film: avoid buying film lying in bright sunlight, check expiry dates.

HEALTH

Insurance
Egypt has well-qualified doctors and good hospitals, particularly in Cairo and Alexandria. Taking out travel insurance which covers medical care is a must. Keep all receipts and medical bills for reimbursement back home.

Dental Services
Have a check-up before leaving home. In an emergency contact your embassy for a list of English-speaking dentists. There are good dentists in Cairo and Alexandria, but make sure you are covered by medical insurance. English-speaking dentist in Cairo: Dr Mohammed A Farao ✉ 7 Sharia Bahal Ahmed Abdel Aziz, Downtown ☎ 02-336 1718

Sun Advice
Use a high factor sunscreen or sunblock, cover up with light cotton clothes, wear sun glasses and a hat when out in the sun. Coffee and alcohol are dehydrating; instead drink plenty of water.

Drugs
Pharmacists (*Saydaliya* in Arabic) usually speak English and can recommend treatment for minor ailments. A wide range of drugs is available over the counter and they are cheap. Check the expiry date and the leaflet to see if it is what you need. Most main cities or resorts have an all-night pharmacy.

Safe Water
It is reasonably safe to drink tap water in the main cities but it is advisable to buy bottles of mineral water, which are widely available. Drink at least 3l of water a day to avoid dehydration from the heat. Avoid ice cubes in drinks.

CONCESSIONS

Students and Youths
Museums and sights offer a 50 per cent reduction on tickets and there are considerable reductions on rail and airline tickets for students who have an official student card. An ISIC Student Card can be issued at the Egyptian Scientific Centre ☎ 23 Sharia el-Manyal above the National Bank, Roda Island, Cairo ☎ 02-531 0330, or at the Ismailiya House (► 100). You need one passport photo and proof that you are a student.

Senior Citizens
There are no special concessions for senior citizens.

CLOTHING SIZES

All these sizes can be found in Egypt, depending on where the clothes have come from

USA	UK	Europe	
36	36	46	**Suits**
38	38	48	
40	40	50	
42	42	52	
44	44	54	
46	46	56	
8	7	41	**Shoes**
8.5	7.5	42	
9.5	8.5	43	
10.5	9.5	44	
11.5	10.5	45	
12	11	46	
14.5	14.5	37	**Shirts**
15	15	38	
15.5	15.5	39/40	
16	16	41	
16.5	16.5	42	
17	17	43	
6	8	34	**Dresses**
8	10	36	
10	12	38	
12	14	40	
14	16	42	
16	18	44	
6	4.5	38	**Shoes**
6.5	5	38	
7	5.5	39	
7.5	6	39	
8	6.5	40	
8.5	7	41	

- Reconfirm your flight two days before departing.
- Arrive at the airport at least two hours before departure time, especially at busy times.
- The duty free shops at Egypt's international airports sell some Egyptian souvenirs, books and postcards and a limited selection of alcohol and perfumes.

LANGUAGE

The official language in Egypt is Arabic, but English is widely taught in schools. People are always happy, and proud, to practise their foreign languages, but even if you only speak a few words in Arabic you will generally meet with an enthusiastic response. Egyptians elaborate their greetings to each other, even on the telephone, and their love of language and for joking with words is legendary in the Arab world. The following is a phonetic transliteration from the Arabic script.

hotel	funduq	hot water	mayya sokhna
single/double room	oda single/ dubbel	shower	dush
		bathroom	hammam
one night	layla wahda	air-conditioning	takyeef
I have a reservation	'andi hagz	telephone	telefun
		key	muftah
can I see the room?	mumkin ashuf el-oda?	lift	ascenseer
		balcony	balacona
is there ...?	fi...?	towel	futa

bank	bank	Egyptian pound	guineh masri
where is the bank?	feen el-bank?	half a pound	nuss guineh
		piastre	irsh
I want to change...	ayyiz/ayza agghayyar... (male/female)	British pound	guineh sterlini
		post office/mail	bosta/barid
		cheque	cheque
money	floos	how much is...?	bi kaam...?

restaurant	mat'am	mineral water	mayya ma'daniya
bon appetit	bi-l-hana wa-sh-shiffa	menu	cart/menu
bill	el-hisab	milk	halib
breakfast	fitaar	salt and pepper	milh wa filfil
tea	shay	wine red, white	nabit ahmar, abyad
coffee	qahwa		
bread	'aysh	beer	beera

right/left	yimeen/shemaal	when does the bus leave?	al-utubees yisaafir emta?
straight ahead	ala toul		
where is...?	feyn...?		
the bus station	mahattat al-utubees	...arrive when?	...yawsal emta?
the train station	mahattat al-atr	Is it far/ near?	da baeed/ urayyib
the airport	el-mataar		
I want a taxi	ayiz/ayza taksi	here/ there	hinna/hinnaak

yes/no	aywa, na'am/ la'a	hello (to Copts)	sa'eeda
		goodbye	ma'a salaama
thank you	shukran	welcome	ahlan wa sahlan
you're welcome	'afwan		
please	min fadlak (to a man), min fadlik (to a woman)	no problem	ma feesh mushkila
		that is too much	da kateeer awi
God willing	inshallah		
hello (to Muslims)	as-salaamu 'alaykum	impossible	mish mumkin
		my name is ...	ismee...

INDEX

Abdin Palace Museum 42
Abu Simbel 82
Abu'l Hol 17
Abydos 16
accommodation 100–105
Aga Khan Mausoleum 76
Agricultural Museum 111
el-Ahram 17
airline services 119, 121
airports 119
Akhenaten 10, 14
el-Qasr 62
el-Alamein 60
alcoholic drinks 57
Al-Qasr 62
Alexandria 45, 51, 52–55, 58–9
Amada 83
Amr ibn El-As Mosque 31
Amud el-Sawari 53
Aqua Park 111
Arabian Horse Stable 110, 115
art galleries 108
Aswan 25, 45, 76–77, 79
Aswan Antiquities Museum 77
el-Azhar Mosque and University 34

Bab Zuwayla 34
baby essentials 111
Bahariya 62
banks 120
Bayt el-Kritiliya 36
Bayt el-Suhaymi 36
Bedouins 98, 109
belly dancing 9, 112
Ben Ezra Synagogue 36
Beni Hasan 74
Biban el-Harim 69
Biban el-Muluk 18
Biban el-Nubalaa 70
Bibliotheca Alexandria 53
birdwatching 12, 13, 45, 46
Birket Qarun 46, 111
Birket Siwa 63
Blue Hole 89
Botanical Gardens 78
Bur Sa'id 86
buses 121

Cairo 22–3, 26, 30–43, 45
Cairo Land 111
Cairo Opera House 37, 113
Cairo Tower 37
camel markets 80
The Canyon 89
car rental 121
Carriage Museum 41
Cavafy Museum 54
children's attractions 110–11
cinema and theatre 113
Citadel, Cairo 41
Cleopatra 14, 53
climate 118
concessions 123
Coptic Museum 40
credit cards 119

customs regulations 119
cycling 114
Dahab 87
Dahshur 46
Dakhla 62
Dandara 74
Daraw 45, 80
Deir Baramus 61
Deir el-Bahari 45, 70, 122
Deir el-Haggar 62
Deir el-Maqar 61
Deir el-Medina 70
Deir el-Suryani 61
Deir Sant Katarin 19
dental services 123
departure information 124
desert 7, 8, 9, 13
desert driving 45, 114
diving and snorkelling 9, 13, 89, 105, 115
Dream Park 111
Dr Ragab's Pharaonic Village 111
drinking water 57, 123
driving 118, 121
drugs and medicines 123

eating out 44–45, 92–99, 110
economy 7
Edfu 80
Egyptian Modern Art, Museum of 37
Egyptian Museum 23, 110
electricity 122
Elephantine Island 78
embassies 120
emergency telephone numbers 119
Esna Temple 81

Farafra 62
El Faiyum 12–13, 46, 111
feluccas 9, 45, 78, 110
festivals and events 116
Fish Garden 111
fishing 45, 114
food and drink 56–57
  see also eating out
food markets 97
football 115

Gawhara Palace 41
Gayer-Anderson House 36
Gezira 37
El-Ghardaqa 90
Giza 9, 17
glass-bottomed boats 110
gliding 114
golf 114–15
El-Gouna 90
Graeco-Roman Museum 58
Green Hole 89

handicrafts 108–109
Hanging Church 40
health 118, 123
Heliopolis 48
High Dam 79

hiking 45
history of Egypt 10–11
horse-racing 115
horse riding 45, 110, 115
hot air ballooning 45
Hurghada 90

Ibn Tulun Mosque 37
insurance 118, 123
Islamic Art, Museum of 38
Islamic Ceramics Museum 38
Isma'iliya 86

El-Kahira see Cairo
Kalabsha 83
Karnak 9, 20–1
Khan el-Khalili 22
Kharga 63
Kitchener's Island 78
Kom Aushim 46
Kom el-Dikka 53
Kom el-Shogafa Catacombs 54
Kom Ombo Temple 81

Lake Nasser 12, 24, 65, 79, 82–83
Lake Nasser cruises 103
language 124
Luxor 45, 64, 66–73
Luxor Museum 68
Luxor Temple 67

Ma'bad el-Uqsur 67
Ma'bad Seti 72
Madinat Habu 72
Mahfouz, Naguib 14
Mahmud Khalil Museum 39
Manyal Palace Museum 39
maps
  Alexandria 52
  Cairo 32-3
  Egypt 28–29
  Luxor West Bank 69
markets 45, 97
Mathaf Cavafy 54
El-Mathaf el-Dawli 58
Mathaf el-Athaar 77
El-Mathaf el-Islami 38
Mathaf el-Khafaz el-Islami 38
El-Mathaf el-Masri 23, 110
Mathaf el-Mumia 68, 110
Mathaf el-Nuba 77
El-Mathaf el-Qibti 40
Mathaf el-Uqsur Li-L-Athaar 68
Mathaf Graeco-Roman 58
Mathaf Mahmoud Said 59
Mathaf Mahmud Khalil 39
Mathaf Markib el-Shams 47
Mathaf Qasr el-Manyal 39
measurements and sizes 122, 123
Memnon Colossi 73
Memphis 47
Mersa Matruh 51, 60
El-Mesala el-Naqsa 79
El-Minya 75
Misr el-Gadida 48
Monastery of St Catherine 19

money 119
Mortuary Temple of Hatshepsut 70
Mortuary Temple of Ramses III 72
Mosque of el-Hakim 34, 35
Mosque of el-Nasir 41
Mosque of Muhammad Ali 41
El-Muallaqa 40
El-Muayyad Mosque 34, 35
Mubarak, President Hosni 14
Mummification Museum 68, 110
Muntazah Palace 59
music 106
Mut 62
Muwazaka Tombs 62

Nasser, Gamal Abdel 11, 14
national holidays 120
National Police Museum 41
Naval Museum 59
Nefertiti 14
nightclubs and discos 112
the Nile (el-Nil) 12, 24, 65
Nile cruises 24, 78
Nile Valley 74–81
Nilometer 77
Nubia Museum 77
Nuweiba 87

oases 62–63, 102
Oasis Heritage Museum 62
opening hours 120
Ozymandias 73

passports and visas 118
personal safety 122
pharmacies 120, 123
Philae Temples 25
photography 123
police 119, 122
Pompey's Pillar 53
population 7
Port Said 86
postal services 120, 122
public transport 121

pyramids 17, 46, 48–49
El-Qal'a 41
Qal'at Qaytbay 59
Qalawun, El-Nasir and Barquq Complex 41
Qasr Abdin 42
Qasr el-Muntazah 59
Qasr Ibrim 83
Qaytbay Fort 59
Qaytbay Mausoleum-Madrasa 42
Quseir 90

Railway Museum 110
Ramadan 116
Ramesseum 73
Ras Muhammad 88
Rashid 51, 60–1
Red Sea 9, 89
Red Sea Aquarium 110
Red Sea coast 90
Red Sea mountains 13, 90
Roman Odeon 53
Rommel Museum 60
Rosetta 51, 60–1
Rosetta Stone 61
Royal Jewellery Museum 58-9

El-Sadd el-Ali 79
St Simeon's Monastery 78
Salah el-Din 88
Saqqara 48–49
Sayyidna el-Husayn Mosque 43
Seized Museum 41
senior citizens 123
Shark Observatory 89
Sharm el-Sheikh 88
shopping 106–109, 120
Sinai 13, 19, 85, 87–88, 89
Sindbad Submarine 110
Siwa 63
Sohag 51
Solar Boat Museum 47
souks 9, 22, 45, 107
Sphinx 17
sports and activities 45, 114–15
students and youths 123

Suez Canal 85, 86
Sultan Hasan Mosque-Madrasa 26
sun protection 123
swimming 45

Taba 88
taxis 121
telephones 122
Tell el-Amarna 75
Temple of Hathor 74
Temple of Horus 80
Temple of Seti I 72
Thebes 66
time differences 118, 119
tipping 122
toilets 121
tourist offices 118, 120
trains 121
travel arrangements 119
travel documents 118
travellers' cheques 119
Tuna el-Gebel 75
Tutankhamun 10, 14, 18, 23

Unfinished Obelisk 79

Valley of the Kings 18
Valley of the Nobles 70
Valley of the Queens 69

Wadi Natrun 61
Wadi el-Sebu'a 83
Wadi Rayan 46
walks
  Alexandria 55
  Cairo 35
War Museum 60
Western Desert 13, 62
Whirling Dervishes 113
White Desert 62
Wikalat el-Ghuri 43
windsurfing 45
Workers' Village 70
World Trade Centre 107
wreck diving 105
Wust el-Balad 43

Acknowledgements

The Automobile Association wishes to thank the following photographers and libraries for their assistance in the preparation of this book.

JAMES MORRIS/AXIOM 35b, 90; BRUCE COLEMAN COLLECTION 89b; MARY EVANS PICTURE LIBRARY 10/11; PAUL STERRY/NATURE PHOTOGRAPHERS 12b; SPECTRUM COLOUR LIBRARY 41, 66b.

The remaining photographs (including the cover photograph) are held in the Association's own library (AA WORLD TRAVEL LIBRARY) and were taken by Rick Strange with the exception of the following: HUGH ALEXANDER 6, 31; CHRIS COE 1, 5a, 5b, 6a, 7a, 7b, 8a, 9a, 10, 11, 12a, 14a, 14b, 15a, 16a, 17a, 17b, 18a, 19a, 19b, 20a, 21a, 22a, 23a, 23b, 23c, 24a, 25a, 26a, 26b, 27b, 34, 36b, 38b, 39b, 40b, 42b, 45b, 46b, 49b, 50, 52b, 54b, 57b, 58b, 62b, 65, 66a, 67, 68a, 69, 70, 71, 72, 73a, 73b, 74a, 75a, 77, 78a, 79a, 79b, 80a, 81a, 82a, 83a, 83b, 85, 87a, 88a, 89a, 117a, 117b, 122a.

Authors' Acknowledgements

The authors would like to thank the following for their help during the research of this book:
Mme Samia Khafaga of the Egyptian State Tourist Office, London; Mr Sabri, Inspector of Antiquities, West Bank, Luxor; Siona Jenkins and Mr Wagdy Soliman of Soliman Travel, London.

Revision Management: Apostrophe S Limited   **Copy editor:** Anne Heseltine

Dear Essential Traveller

Your comments, opinions and recommendations are very important to us. So please help us to improve our travel guides by taking a few minutes to complete this simple questionnaire.

You do not need a stamp (unless posted outside the UK). If you do not want to cut this page from your guide, then photocopy it or write your answers on a plain sheet of paper.

Send to: **The Editor, AA World Travel Guides, FREEPOST SCE 4598, Basingstoke RG21 4GY.**

Your recommendations…

We always encourage readers' recommendations for restaurants, nightlife or shopping – if your recommendation is used in the next edition of the guide, we will send you a ***FREE*** AA ***Essential*** **Guide** of your choice. Please state below the establishment name, location and your reasons for recommending it.

_____

_____

_____

_____

Please send me **AA *Essential*** _____

About this guide…

Which title did you buy?
    AA *Essential* _____
Where did you buy it?_____
When? m m / y y

Why did you choose an AA *Essential* Guide? _____

_____

_____

_____

Did this guide meet your expectations?
    Exceeded ☐   Met all ☐   Met most ☐   Fell below ☐
    Please give your reasons_____

_____

_____

_____

continued on next page…

Were there any aspects of this guide that you particularly liked? _____

_____

_____

Is there anything we could have done better? _____

_____

_____

About you...

Name (*Mr/Mrs/Ms*) _____

   Address _____

_____

   _____ Postcode _____

Daytime tel nos _____

Please only give us your mobile phone number if you wish to hear from us about other products and services from the AA and partners by text or mms.

Which age group are you in?
   Under 25 ☐ 25–34 ☐ 35–44 ☐ 45–54 ☐ 55–64 ☐ 65+ ☐

How many trips do you make a year?
   Less than one ☐ One ☐ Two ☐ Three or more ☐

Are you an AA member? Yes ☐ No ☐

About your trip...

When did you book? m m / y y   When did you travel? m m / y y

How long did you stay? _____

Was it for business or leisure? _____

Did you buy any other travel guides for your trip?

   If yes, which ones? _____

Thank you for taking the time to complete this questionnaire. Please send it to us as soon as possible, and remember, you do not need a stamp (*unless posted outside the UK*).

Happy Holidays!

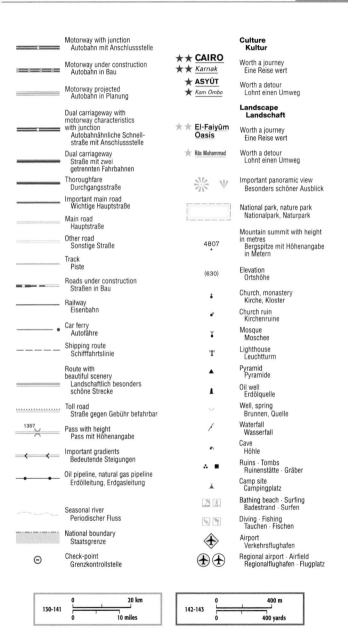

Motorway with junction
Autobahn mit Anschlussstelle

Motorway under construction
Autobahn in Bau

Motorway projected
Autobahn in Planung

Dual carriageway with
motorway characteristics
with junction
Autobahnähnliche Schnell-
straße mit Anschlussstelle

Dual carriageway
Straße mit zwei
getrennten Fahrbahnen

Thoroughfare
Durchgangsstraße

Important main road
Wichtige Hauptstraße

Main road
Hauptstraße

Other road
Sonstige Straße

Track
Piste

Roads under construction
Straßen in Bau

Railway
Eisenbahn

Car ferry
Autofähre

Shipping route
Schifffahrtslinie

Route with
beautiful scenery
Landschaftlich besonders
schöne Strecke

Toll road
Straße gegen Gebühr befahrbar

1357 Pass with height
Pass mit Höhenangabe

Important gradients
Bedeutende Steigungen

Oil pipeline, natural gas pipeline
Erdölleitung, Erdgasleitung

Seasonal river
Periodischer Fluss

National boundary
Staatsgrenze

Check-point
Grenzkontrollstelle

Culture
Kultur

★★ **CAIRO**
★★ _Karnak_

Worth a journey
Eine Reise wert

★ **ASYÛT**
★ _Kom Ombo_

Worth a detour
Lohnt einen Umweg

Landscape
Landschaft

★★ El-Faiyûm
Oasis

Worth a journey
Eine Reise wert

★ Râs Muhammad

Worth a detour
Lohnt einen Umweg

Important panoramic view
Besonders schöner Ausblick

National park, nature park
Nationalpark, Naturpark

4807

Mountain summit with height
in metres
Bergspitze mit Höhenangabe
in Metern

(630)

Elevation
Ortshöhe

Church, monastery
Kirche, Kloster

Church ruin
Kirchenruine

Mosque
Moschee

Lighthouse
Leuchtturm

Pyramid
Pyramide

Oil well
Erdölquelle

Well, spring
Brunnen, Quelle

Waterfall
Wasserfall

Cave
Höhle

Ruins · Tombs
Ruinenstätte · Gräber

Camp site
Campingplatz

Bathing beach · Surfing
Badestrand · Surfen

Diving · Fishing
Tauchen · Fischen

Airport
Verkehrsflughafen

Regional airport · Airfield
Regionalflughafen · Flugplatz

130-141   0   20 km
          0   10 miles

142-143   0   400 m
          0   400 yards

Maps © Mairs Geographischer Verlag / Falk Verlag, 73751 Ostfildern

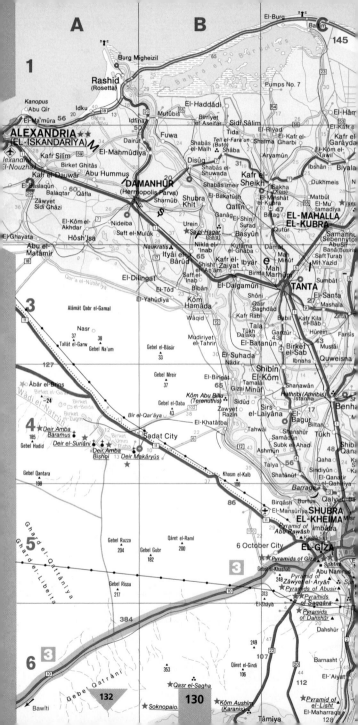

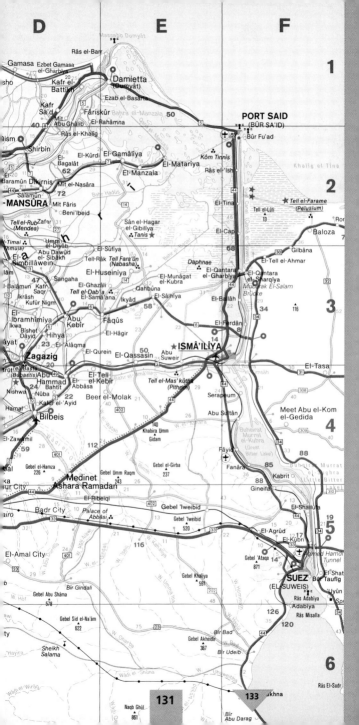

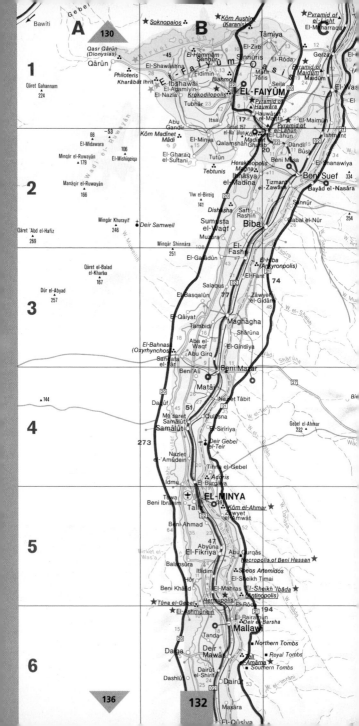

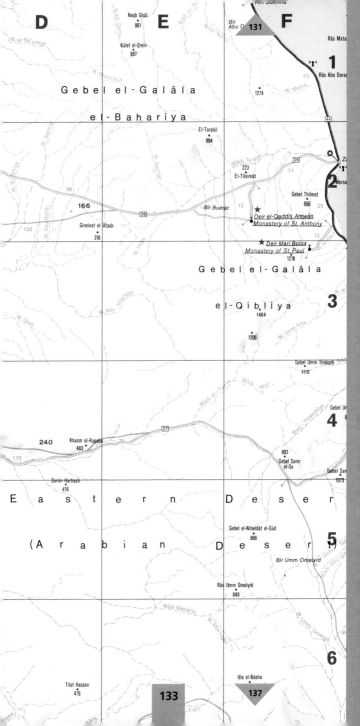

Naqb Ghûl
861

Kület el-Qrein
897

Gebel el-Galâla

el-Bahariya

Âïn Sukhna

Bîr
Abu D   **131**

Râs Mata

1

Râs Abu Dara

65   W. Maina

1274

44

El-Tarabil
994

Za

Wâdi 'Araba

223
El-Tileimât

26

34

2

Mersa

98

166

Bîr Buerât

12

Gebel Thilmet
656

25

Gineinet el-Atash
318

26

★ Deir el-Qaddîs Antwân
Monastery of St. Anthony

15

★ Deir Mari Bolos
Monastery of St. Paul
1218

130

W. Abu Rimth

Gebel el-Galâla

el-Qíbliya
1464

3

W. el

1206

W. Quis

W. Abu

W. Khataga

W. Has

Gebel Umm Tinâssib
1110

W. Umm Arta

Wâdi Mur

Wâdi el-Tarfa

Gebel Un
9

4

240

27

Khasm el-Ragaba
483

170

893
Gebel Samr
el-Qa

Gebel San
1073

Qurûn Harhash
416

E   a   s   t   e   r   n   D   e   s   e   r

Gebel el-Niheidât el-Süd
866

(A   r   a   b   i   a   n   D   e   s   e   r

5

Bîr Umm Omeiyid

Râs Umm Omeiyid
849

Wâdi Mahâriq

W. Abu

W. Umm Omeiyid

6

Tilat Hassan
476

133

Itla el-Bâsha
137

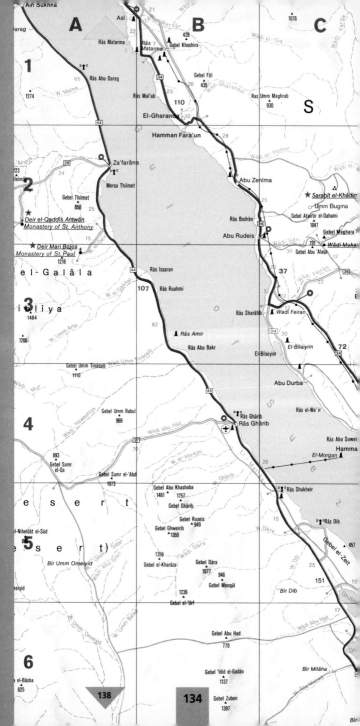

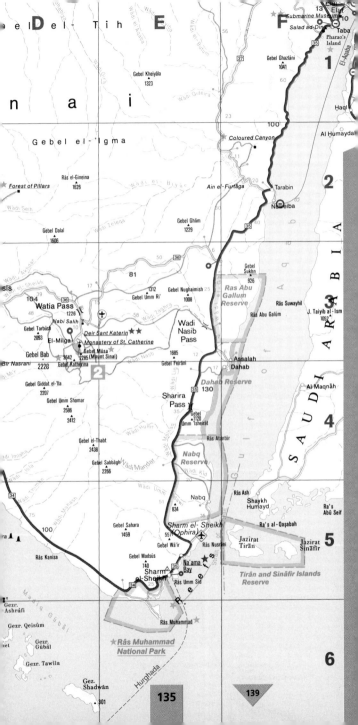

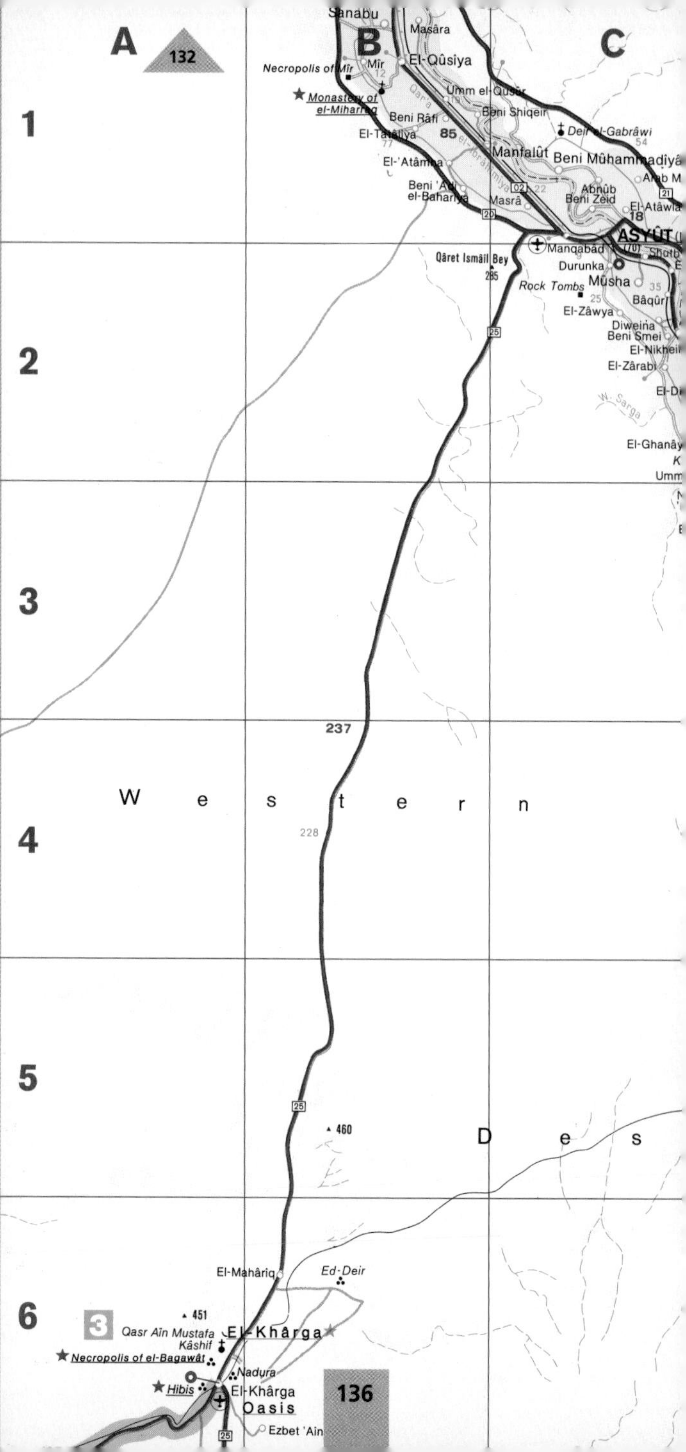

132

Sanabu
Masâra
B
El-Qûsiya
Necropolis of Mîr
Mîr
12
Umm el-Qusûr
★ Monastery of
el-Muharraq
Beni Râfi
Beni Shiqeir
El-Tahâliya 85
Deir el-Gabrâwi 54
Manfalût Beni Mûhammadiya
El-'Atâmna
Beni 'Adi
el-Baharîya
C
Beni Mûhammadiya
Masrâ
02 22
Abnûb
Beni Zeid
Arab M.
21
El-Atâwla
20
18
Qâret Ismâïl Bey
285
Manqabâd
ASYÛT
70
Durunka
Shutb
Rock Tombs
Mûsha
25
Bâqûr
El-Zâwya
Diweina
25
Beni Smei
El-Nikheil
El-Zârabi
El-D
W. Sarga
El-Ghanây
K
Umm
N
E

237

W   e   s   t   e   r   n

228

25
★ 460

D   e   s

El-Mahâriq
Ed-Deir

3
451
Qasr Aïn Mustafa
Kâshif
El-Khârga ★
★ Necropolis of el-Bagawât
Nadura
★ Hibis
El-Khârga
Oasis
136
Ezbet 'Ain
25

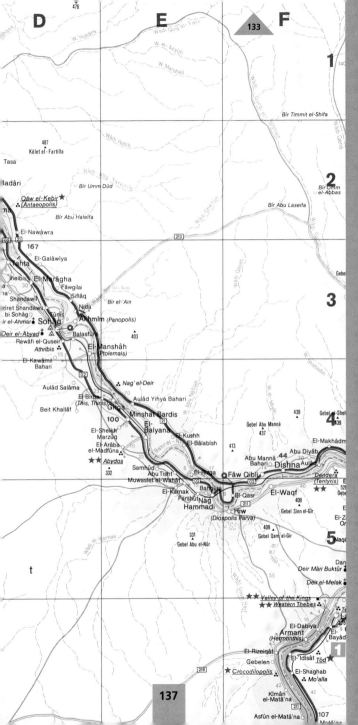

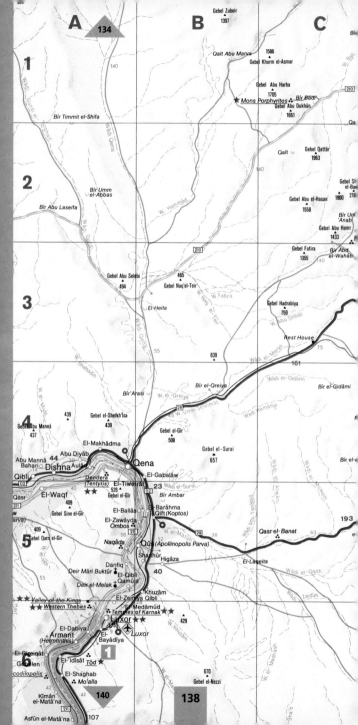

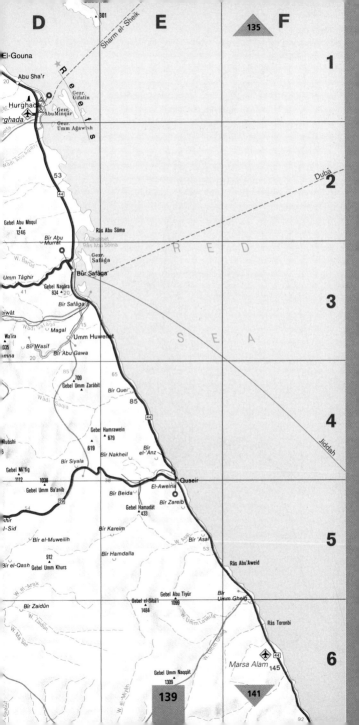

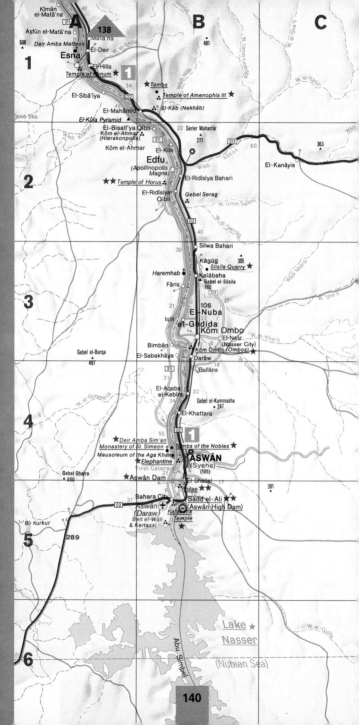

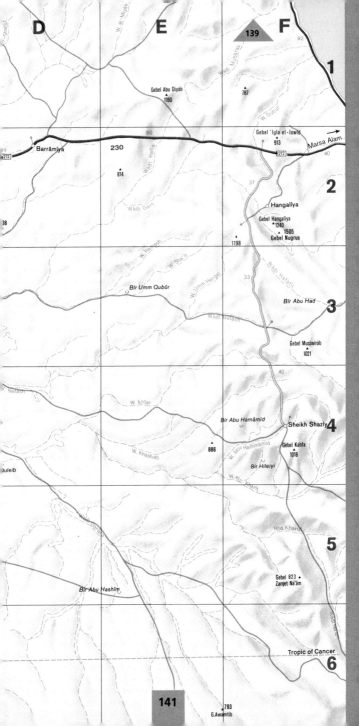

W. el-Miyáh

Wádi Mubárak

92

1

Gebel Abu Diyáb
▲1160

▲787

W. Dubur

80

Gebel 'Igla el-Iswid
▲913

Marsa Alam

Barrâmîya

212

230

Wádi Hafia

40

212

▲814

37

2

Wádi Gart

Hangalîya

Gebel Hangaliya
▲1240
▲1505
Gebel Nugrus

▲1198

W. Hameish

W. Sha'ît

W. Umm Hargal

Wádi Harafit

33

Bir Umm Qubûr

Wádi Natash

Bir Abu Had

3

Gebel Musiwiráb
▲1021

40

W. Natash

W. Antar

Bir Abu Hamámid

Sheikh Shazly

4

W. Khashab

▲886

W. Abu Hammámid

Gebel Kahfa
▲1016

Bir Hileiyi

W. El- Kharit

Juleib

Wádi Shait

Rôd Khanÿ

5

Gebel 823 ▲
Zarqet Na'ám

Bir Abu Hashîm

Tropic of Cancer

6

▲793
G.Awamtib

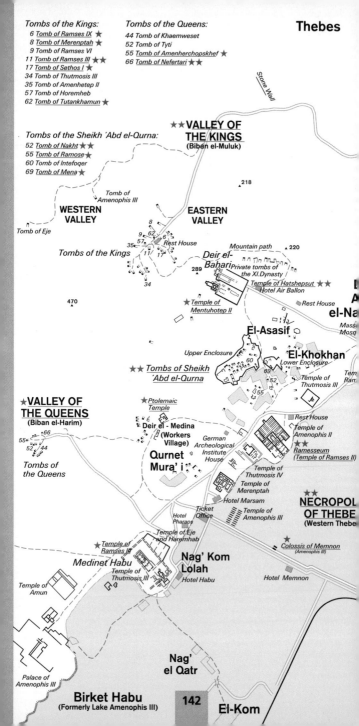

Thebes

Tombs of the Kings:
6 <u>Tomb of Ramses IX</u> ★
8 <u>Tomb of Merenptah</u> ★
9 Tomb of Ramses VI
11 <u>Tomb of Ramses III</u> ★★
17 <u>Tomb of Sethos I</u> ★
34 Tomb of Thutmosis III
35 Tomb of Amenhotep II
57 Tomb of Horemheb
62 <u>Tomb of Tutankhamun</u> ★

Tombs of the Queens:
44 Tomb of Khaemweset
52 Tomb of Tyti
55 <u>Tomb of Amenherchopskhef</u> ★
66 <u>Tomb of Nefertari</u> ★★

Tombs of the Sheikh 'Abd el-Qurna:
52 <u>Tomb of Nakht</u> ★★
55 <u>Tomb of Ramose</u> ★
60 Tomb of Intefoqer
69 <u>Tomb of Mena</u> ★

Stone Wall

★★**VALLEY OF THE KINGS**
(Biban el-Muluk)

▲218

Tomb of Amenophis III

WESTERN VALLEY

EASTERN VALLEY

Tomb of Eje

Tombs of the Kings

8
9 62 6
57
35
11 17
Rest House

34

470 ▲

▲220

Mountain path

289 ▲

Deir el-Bahari
Private tombs of the XI.Dynasty
Temple of Hatshepsut ★★
Hotel Air Ballon

★ *Temple of Mentuhotep II*

Rest House

Masse Mosq

El-Asasif

El-Khokhan

Upper Enclosure

Lower Enclosure

60
52
55
Temple of Thutmosis III

A el-Na

★★ <u>*Tombs of Sheikh 'Abd el-Qurna*</u>

Tem Ran

★**VALLEY OF THE QUEENS**
(Biban el-Harim)

★ *Ptolemaic Temple*

Deir el - Medina
(Workers Village)

German Archeological Institute House

Qurnet Mura' i

Rest House
Temple of Amenophis II

★★
<u>Ramesseum</u>
(Temple of Ramses II)

66
55 52 44

Tombs of the Queens

Temple of Thutmosis IV

Temple of Merenptah

Hotel Marsam

Temple of Amenophis III

★★
NECROPOL OF THEBE
(Western Thebe

Ticket Office

Hotel Pharaos

★ <u>Temple of Ramses III</u>

Medinet Habu

Temple of Eje and Haremhab

Temple of Thutmosis III

Nag' Kom Lolah

Hotel Habu

★
<u>Colossis of Memnon</u>
(Amenophis III)

Hotel Memnon

Temple of Amun

Temple of Amenophis III

Nag' el Qatr

Palace of Amenophis III

Birket Habu
(Formerly Lake Amenophis III)

142

El-Kom

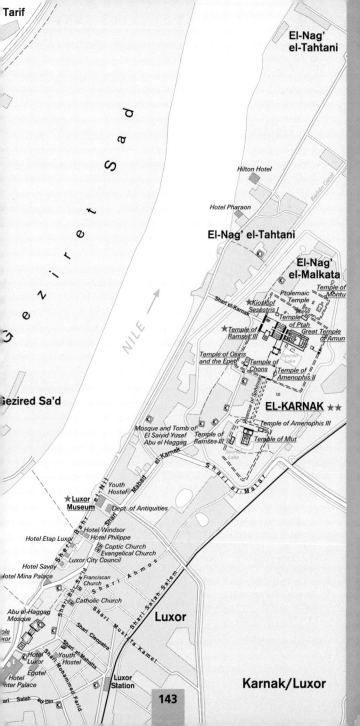

Tarif

El-Nag' el-Tahtani

G e z i r e t   S a d

Hilton Hotel

Hotel Pharaon

El-Nag' el-Tahtani

El-Nag' el-Malkata

Temple of Montu

NILE →

Shari' el-Karnak

★ Kiosk of Sesostris

Ptolemaic Temple

Temple of Ptah

Great Temple of Amun

★ Temple of Ramses III

Temple of Osiris and the Epet

Temple of Chons

Sacred Lake

Temple of Amenophis II

Gezired Sa'd

Avenue of Sphinxes

EL-KARNAK ★★

Temple of Amenophis III

Mosque and Tomb of El Saiyid Yusef Abu el Haggag

Temple of Ramses III

Temple of Mut

Sacred Lake

Shari el-Matar

Mabad   el-Karnak

Shari   Bahr   El-Nil

Youth Hostel

★ Luxor Museum

Dept. of Antiquities

Shari

Hotel Etap Luxor

Hotel Windsor
Hotel Philippe

Coptic Church
Evangelical Church

Luxor City Council

Hotel Savoy

Franciscan Church

Hotel Mina Palace

Shari   Ahmos

Catholic Church

Abu el-Haggag Mosque

Shari   Abdul Hamid

Shari   Mustafa   Kamel

Shari   Salah   Salem

Luxor

ple xor

Shari Cleopatra

Hotel Luxor

Shari el-Mahatta

Youth Hostel

Shari   Mohammed-Farid

Luxor Station

Egotel

nter Palace

ari   Salah   ed Din

Karnak/Luxor

143

Sight Locator Index

This index relates to the atlas section on pages 130–43. We have given map references to the main sights of interest in the book. Some sights in the index may not be plotted on the atlas. Note: ibc – inside back cover. Ifc – inside front cover.

Abu Simbel off 140B6
Abydos 137D4
Aga Khan Mausoleum 140B4
el-Ahram & Abu'l Hol (Pyramids & Sphinx) 130C5/6
Alexandria 130A1
Amud el-Sawari (Pompey's Pillar) 130A1
Aswan 140B4
el-Azhar Mosque and University ibcE3
Bab Zuwayla ibcE4
Bahariya ifc
Bayt el-Kritiliya (Gayer-Anderson House) ibcE5
Bayt el-Suhaymi ibcF3
Ben Ezra Synagogue off ibcC6
Beni Hasan 132B5
Biban el-Harim (Valley of the Queens) 142
Biban el-Muluk (Valley of the Kings) 142
Biban el-Nubalaa (Valley of the Nobles) 142
Cairo ibc, 130C5
Dahshur 130C6
Dakhla ifc
Dandara, Temple of Hathor 138A4
Daraw 140B5
Deir el-Bahari (Mortuary Temple of Hatshepsut) 142
Deir el-Medina (Workers' Village) 142
Deir Sant Katarin (St Catherine's Monastery) 135E3
Edfu (Temple of Horus) 140B2
Esna Temple 140A1

el-Faiyum 132B1
Farafra ifc
Gezira, Cairo ibcB3
Ibn Tulun Mosque ibcD5
Kalabsha 140B5
Karnak 143
Kham el-Khalili ibcE3
Kharga ifc
Kom el-Dikka (Roman Odeon) 130A1
Kom el-Shogafa Catacombs 130A1
Kom Ombo Temple 140B3
Lake Nasser 140B6
Luxor 143
Ma'bad el-Uqsur (Luxor Temple) 143
Ma'bad Seti (Temple of Seti I) 138A6
Madinet Habu (Mortuary Temple of Ramses III) 142
Mathaf el-Athaar (Aswan Antiquities Museum) 140B4
El-Mathaf el-Dawli (National Museum of Alexandria) 130A1
Mathaf el-Islami (Museum of Islamic Art) ibcE3
Mathaf el-Khafaz el-Islami (Islamic Ceramics Museum) ibcB2
Mathaf el-Masri (Egyptian Museum) ibcC3
Mathaf el-Mumia (Mummification Museum) 138A6
Mathaf el-Nuba (Nubia Museum) 140B4
Mathaf el-Qibiti (Coptic Museum) off ibcC6
El Mathaf el-Romani (Graeco-Roman

Museum) 130A1
Mathaf el-Uqsur li-l-Athaar (Luxor Museum) 143
Mathaf Mahmud Khalil (Mahmud Khalil Museum) ibcB4
Mathaf Markib el-Shams (Solar Boat Museum) 130C5
Memnon Colossi 142
Memphis 130C5
el-Nil (the Nile) ifc
Philae Temples 140B5
el-Qal'a (Citadel) ibcE5
Qal'at Qaytbay (Qaytbay Fort) 130A1
Qalawun, el-Nasir and Barquq Complex ibcE3
Qasr Abdin (Abdin Palace Museum) ibcD4
Qasr el-Muntazah (Muntazah Palace) 130A1
Qasr Ibrim off 140B6
Qaytbay Mausoleum-Madrasa, Cairo ibcF4
Ramesseum 142
Ras Muhammad 135E6
Sadd el-Ali (High Dam) 140B5
Saqqara 130C5
Sharm el-Sheikh 135E5
Sinai 134–35
Siwa ifc
Suez Canal 131F2/3
Sultan Hasan Mosque-Madrasa ibcE5
Tell el-Amarna 132B6
Tuna el-Gebel 132B5
Wadi el-Natrun 130A4
Wadi el-Sebu'a 140B6
Wikalat el-Ghuri ibcE3
Wust el-Balad (Downtown) ibcC4

For the main index see pages 125–26